THE MONTREAL MASSACRE

THE MONTREAL MASSACRE

EDITED BY **LOUISE MALETTE** AND **MARIE CHALOUH**
TRANSLATED BY **MARLENE WILDEMAN**

gynergy books, 1991

Cover painting: *The Hidden War,* by Sheree-Lee Olson
English-language editing: Lynn Henry
Book design: Lynn Henry
Printing: Les Ateliers Graphiques Marc Veilleux Inc.

With thanks to the Canada Council for its kind support

gynergy books
P.O. Box 2023
Charlottetown,
Prince Edward Island
C1A 7N7

Canadian Cataloguing in Publication Data
   The Montreal massacre
      Translation of: Polytechnique, 6 décembre.
      ISBN 0-921881-14-2
   1. Women—Crimes against. 2. École polytechnique
   (Montreal, Quebec)—Massacre, 1989. 3. Mass murder—Quebec
   (Province)—Montreal. 4. Sex discrimination against women.
   I. Malette, Louise. II. Chalouh, Marie.
   HV6535.C33M6513 1991   305.42′09714′28   C91-097528-0

Printed and bound in Canada on 50% recycled paper

Contents

This book is dedicated to the memory of the victims of the December 6, 1989 massacre

Publisher's Note

Why publish an English-language edition of a book about the reaction in Quebec to the 1989 massacre of fourteen women at an engineering school, the Ecole Polytechnique, in Montreal?

In their Preface to the English Edition, the editors of the original French-language book give three compelling answers to this question. In essence, their words reiterate what the contents of this book testify to and what we, as the English-language publisher, know to be true: the massacre of fourteen women on December 6, 1989, was not the isolated act of a madman but a horrifying reflection of misogyny in our society. As such it engages our deepest emotions and demands examination.

Moreover, the reaction in Quebec, and specifically in the French-language media, is of great interest because it differs from reaction in the English-language media. Several essays and articles in this book examine this issue, addressing the question of why denial and censorship of specifically feminist analysis of the massacre was so powerful, even as Québécois society groped for explanations. While the mainstream media scrambled to ignore or downplay the significance of the victims being women, the analysis of feminists was ignored or ridiculed or rejected with hostility.

Much of the writing in the pages that follow found a readership only through the publication of this book. These writings are a testament to the immediate pain and grief felt by their authors and, even more importantly, to the strength and courage of voices compelled to speak hard truths. While the English-language media, perhaps because of its relative distance from the event, allowed more information to filter through to the public, it too lacked the courage to step out of its role as the reflector of an essentially misogynist and patriarchal point of view.

Such denial is ironic in the light of subsequent events. As much as the mainstream media would like to isolate the massacre as an aberrant incident in time and place, it continues to affect us. A little less than a year after the killings, in November of 1990, columnist Francine Pelletier of the Montreal daily, *La Presse*, was sent, anonymously, the suicide letter of mass murderer Marc Lépine. After much discussion, we have decided to include the letter in this edition of the book. This was a difficult decision. It is not our intention to produce a book, apologist or otherwise, about the murderer. As much as the Montreal massacre is not an act isolated in time and place, it is also an act not isolated to one man. Indeed, for these reasons, some of the contributors to this book have chosen to represent the killer by his initials, M.L., rather than his full name. We feel that the letter, somewhat ironically (for this was certainly not the killer's intention), reinforces in our minds the courage and truthfulness with which the writers in this book speak out about violence against women.

One further change from the French-language edition is the addition of information about the women who were killed (although reference is often made to the fourteen students, not all of the women who died were students). Again and again in the writings that follow we come back to them, as we must come back to them as a society—and it is to them that this book is dedicated.

Some readers will be surprised, upon opening this book, to find their names in the Table of Contents. They wrote letters to certain newspapers, who subsequently gave us permission to reprint them in this collection. We would have liked to personally contact each one of these individuals prior to publication, but for reasons too obvious to recount here, we were able to trace but a few.

We wish to thank all those who wrote letters for having had the courage of their convictions. To publicize differing or unpopular opinions requires a good deal of courage. To have reacted, to have made a gesture—to have thought about what happened and written a letter that may or may not be published, to have asked oneself "What's the use?" and put the letter in the mailbox anyway, to have waited and watched the editorial pages . . . all these actions indicate to us that these people have responded to a flicker of hope deep inside, and only hope can spark courage. May those who signed their names to these letters know their efforts were not in vain. Theirs are some of the most discerning points of view considered for this book. Gathered together here, they will be preserved for the informative invaluable documents they truly are.

Once again, we wish to thank all of them for having passed along the kind of hope so necessary for accomplishing this project.

Louise Malette

Preface to the English Edition

There is no doubt about the relevance of this English edition. In the first place, despite the passage of time since its original publication, the contents of this collection are unfortunately still highly topical. The Quebec news media has managed to provide us with numerous occasions to draw parallels between the massacre at the Polytechnique and endemic domestic violence. By and large, the press dealt with these situations, but mainly as "news-in-brief", and sometimes with a certain sensationalism. Never was domestic violence linked to women's traditional fate. It was attributed to poverty, unemployment, insanity—never to misogyny. Public acknowledgement of the connection, however, would be the key to developing new values and constructing a new world. For this reason, the authors of this book have uniformly exposed, reflected upon and denounced this misogyny.

Next, the profound reflection warranted by an event like the massacre at the Polytechnique does not appear to be taking place in Quebec. A year after this book was first published in French, we would like to claim that it in some way contributed to raising people's consciousness or to provoking the profound reflection that stimulates widespread public debate. This, we know, is necessary if a change in mentality is to come about. Alas, we are unable to make such a claim. To be sure, the book's appearance in April 1990 was politely recognized by the critical establishment, which, despite a certain embarrassment, was content to make only a cursory perusal of its contents. And then this obviously disturbing book was quickly forgotten.

Finally, the very existence of this book is like soothing balm on a still raw wound, and though such consolation might be minimal considering the pain women feel, it is only right and just that it be shared.

Louise Malette

Preface

Deciding to work on publishing a book that would analyze the tragedy at the Polytechnique was a bit like putting one's foot in a door that was about to close. But if, in the weaving of individual existence, there are times when forgetting is therapeutic, for women there are times when remembering is imperative. We come together through remembering, and we see ourselves and each other in our own history. Whether we like it or not, the massacre at the Polytechnique is now part of our history.

A concrete addition to that grievous memory, this book offers a profound understanding of what happened—personal and political reflections which will contribute indispensable perspectives to the public debate we hope to see take place.

In this way we remember, understand and make change. Change must come, for if, in the final analysis, this tragedy is a landmark in the history of the relations between the sexes, it also reveals the urgent necessity to combat the opppressive structure that props up these relationships.

Feminist claims for equality are much more than a question of numbers and statistics; they are a matter of justice. Yes, justice with a capital "J." It becomes imperative to radically alter our world view and we are convinced, now more than ever, that it will be the fundamental values of women that will bring about this transformation.

Louise Malette
Marie Chalouh

Here, in alphabetical order, are the names of the fourteen women who were killed on December 6, 1989 at the University of Montreal's school of engineering, the Polytechnique.

GENEVIÈVE BERGERON, twenty-one, was a second-year scholarship student in civil engineering.

HÉLÈNE COLGAN, twenty-three, was in her final year of mechanical engineering and planned to take her master's degree.

NATHALIE CROTEAU, twenty-three, was in her final year of mechanical engineering.

BARBARA DAIGNEAULT, twenty-two, was in her final year of mechanical engineering and held a teaching assistantship.

ANNE-MARIE EDWARD, twenty-one, was a first-year student in chemical engineering.

MAUD HAVIERNICK, twenty-nine, was a second-year student in engineering materials, a branch of metallurgy, and a graduate in environmental design.

BARBARA MARIA KLUCZNIK, thirty-one, was a second-year engineering student specializing in engineering materials.

MARYSE LAGANIÈRE, twenty-five, worked in the budget department of the Polytechnique.

MARYSE LECLAIR, twenty-three, was a fourth-year student in engineering materials.

ANNE-MARIE LEMAY, twenty-seven, was a fourth-year student in mechanical engineering.

SONIA PELLETIER, twenty-eight, was to graduate the next day in mechanical engineering. She was awarded a degree posthumously.

MICHÈLE RICHARD, twenty-one, was a second-year student in engineering materials.

ANNIE ST-ARNEAULT, twenty-three, was a mechanical engineering student.

ANNIE TURCOTTE, twenty-one, was a first-year student in engineering materials.

THE IDEAL SITE FOR THE CRIME

Louky Bersianik

"To be sure, in the world of male fantasy, woman's body serves as the ideal site for the crime."

Alain Robbe-Grillet

Maud, 29 years

Hélène, 23 years

Nathalie, 23 years

Geneviève, 21 years

Michèle, 21 years

Sonia, 28 years

Anne-Marie, 21 years

THE IDEAL SITE FOR THE CRIME

Annie, 21 years

Maryse, 23 years

Barbara, 22 years

Anne-Marie, 27 years

Barbara, 31 years

Maryse, 25 years

Annie, 23 years

I

To the child alive and well
caught up in her thoughts
obliquely
on this Monday with things to do
she heads toward the lot
where Sunday she'll be laid to rest

There is an evil person
who loves you
don't look now
he's coming from far away
to meet up with you
he knows
you're not afraid of him

His heart brand new
the brain eaten away
by twenty-five years of hatred
he's coming closer
a hero
for your calm youth

In exactly two days
you'll be cut to pieces
by an heroic double-edged sword
this is a first move
a prelude to love

a few little bites
in your life line and
the shattered membrane shocked
spurts forth
your thoughtful look
your joy no going back

uninterrupted cascade
all your blood
welling to the surface

II

To Tuesday's student
massacred Wednesday
buried Thursday

Don't stop to pick
the too red
December crocuses

There is a young man who loves you
clothed in white terror
Don't rush to meet him
Don't tremble when he sees you

He's only after dread
He has one desire only
to see pure terror
rise in your eyes

This young man is a flame-thrower
he will reduce you to ashes
before the day is out

He wants only
to catch your breath
between the pages of night
put it on the cross Friday
forget it Saturday
leafing through
the frozen specks of his
short memory

meanwhile your brief life
oozes like childhood
around the edge of your dreams
which he will have taken from you
without asking

III

To the young woman of the morning
who will be mowed down
at five in the evening
her place is marked already
under snow that flies up
behind her muted step

you will be carried to the earth
in a car like dark water
filed in thought
since the dawn of your meeting
among this scarlet week's
cut roses

There is a jackal who loves you
dangerously
He wants to touch your heart
and today makes ready
to riddle it with bullets

Yesterday he tried to close
the threshold of your flesh
with the iron padlock
of his iron love
and on your youthful body
like on an antique chest
he almost placed the seals

You are his shadow
cast for all eternity
no matter what

His fierce love
is phosphorescent
in the day's opaque light

It's you or him
It's your life against his
It's your heart against his

IV

To the schoolgirl of late morning
quietly writing
who will die a violent death
that afternoon
reciting
her adulterated history lesson

Be careful
There is a boy who loves you
helplessly
You are in danger

He is born of man without end
born of haunted night
determined to destroy you
since your very first day

Your body
is the privileged portion of space
he chose
to annihilate
He gave himself the mission
to rid the species
of your tenacious existence

You are in danger
in your classroom
as the setting sun glints
off your cheek

He is the secret weapon
that bursts into the room
and before the blackboard
engineers
the fatal blow
the fall
for ever and ever

He forbids you ever
to go through this door
the way your brother can,
the heart beating

NO MOTIVE FOR THE CRIME?

The Political is Personal

Nicole Lacelle

For Monique Simard
that her name be erased from the list[1]

The first thing I felt upon hearing the news about the Polytechnique massacre was that this was a case of mistaken identity. Why them and not me? Why not us, those of us who've been feminists for twenty years? We were fully conscious of the hatred our actions provoked, and of the dangers which often threatened us. Why take it out on young women who would never have imagined there could be negative implications to what they were doing? They innocently inherited the career openings we feminists, fully aware of what we were doing, created for women. Why take it out on them, on those "civilians," and not us militants? Simply because they followed in our footsteps? They were so far behind that they'd lost sight of us. For them, it was all very simple—they wanted to become engineers, that's all. It was there for them, available, as long as they came up with the academic and personal effort normally expected to accomplish such a goal. For us it was different, we were on enemy territory, shells exploding around us from all directions; it didn't take much to figure out there was a war going on. These young women ended up standing in No Man's Land; it was only too easy to ignore that the peace treaty had never been signed.

I don't doubt for a moment that my reaction would have been different if they had been politically-aware feminists. I'm sure I would have been furious, outraged, ravaged by violent emotions. Instead I was completely devastated, desolated, by an indescribable sadness. I would have been the raging feminist militant, but there I was, a weeping mother. I felt closer to their mothers than to their friends at school. This was partly due to age, of course—it's only natural.

He was their age, himself. In the grandest political ignorance, his list contained the names of women both feminist and not feminist. Evidently he considered them all beyond his reach, so he turned to his own generation. What was he thinking of, that child? What was going through his mind, once he had discarded all those publicly-recognizable representatives of women's consciousness in the world? Did he think it was a holy war? Did he think that once he'd destroyed the enemies of his religion, he'd go up to heaven, glorious? (Would this image have occurred to me if his Arabic origins hadn't been divulged? I honestly don't think so, but in any case I don't find it more apt; Northern demons are no more beautiful, and the result would have been just as sinister.) He had to put a name to what he was doing, regardless, and in so doing he embarrassed our great thinkers who would have liked, without this hindrance, to interpret the event to their liking. He had to name feminism in order to give meaning to his act, he absolutely had to have his act mean something. And that devastated us. But let's look at the asinine comments such as "our youth is beyond the pale," i.e. it's something that happened between our young men and women, and they're the ones who are going to have to deal with it. It is horrifying that, in societies capable of putting a man on the Moon, people actually think that the murdering of women can make sense—that being caught in the flagrant misdemeanor of being "woman" can give murder a reason. I say "woman," not feminist. One among them even said, "We are not feminists," and she was right to say so for, subjectively at least, this was true. For him, it seems there wasn't any difference, as though he had said to them, "You are acting like feminists, and you are in a place that should be forbidden to women, so you are feminists." Obviously, for him, the fine line wasn't necessary; he skipped it, just as in most of our society people want to avoid the challenge of political issues, avoid thinking, and sometimes avoid words themselves, seeing them as useless and annoying labels. We would like so much to ignore these challenges. And then we're surprised that our young people are not motivated to learn to read and write properly. We are surprised that the feminists "take advantage of" what happened at the Polytechnique. All of a sudden, the women say to themselves: if it really was women who were singled out, I could have been one of them. All of a sudden, the men say to themselves: it was a man who fired that gun, and we too are men. It all happened deep in the unconscious, everyone pursuing their own objectives in utter darkness, right up to the fatal collision. Fourteen women dead, and one man. How many wounded?

Now obviously we're not talking about blame here. As one woman student said at a press conference: "Only one person was guilty, and he's dead." Social solidarity does exist but it is not a borderless amoeba colony. And it is not a matter of feeling guilty, which is to come to a dead stop, but a matter of learning something—progressing. It is not a matter of confusing ethics with conscience. I'm talking about *having* a conscience, and about those incredible unconscious forces which can take over, if ever we cease that rigorous dialogue we maintain with the self and the world. We had no idea how true it was when we said in 1968: "If you don't get political, politics will get you."

Somehow I manage to think there might have been a lesbian in one of those classes that afternoon, flat on her stomach like the others, but whose life was saved because of her short hair. The young lunatic, caught up in his exaggerated notions of femininity, would have mistaken her for a guy. Her tendency to avoid confrontations with men, her disregard for whether or not men like her, her desire to be herself and to make no effort to attract them, is what would have saved her life. If she exists somewhere, I hope she is not alone as she ponders all this. I am crying with her, and I cry the same tears she does.

Some days after the killing, another woman student at the Polytechnique said on television that it was true most of the women students were not feminists, that most of her friends, men and women, took the presence of women at the Polytechnique for granted, that they had never felt the need to stop and examine this, but incidents such as this one meant that it would no longer be possible for them to side-step the issue. The personal is political, we used to say; maybe it is time to invert the proposition, make the political become personal, take it to heart, let our developing thoughts about it mean something. In the general uproar over control of firearms is anybody listening to this woman student's voice protesting that they weren't feminists? It goes without saying that getting hold of a gun must be made more difficult. But it is not a rifle that pulls the trigger, it is a human being, usually a man. And it's not a human being who dies, it's a woman.

Notes

1. The name of Monique Simard, Vice-President of a Quebec union, the CSN, was on the hit list of the murderer. (Editor's note)

The Killer was no Young Man

Nicole Brossard

*This article appeared in La Presse, on December 21, 1989, and was later published in **The Amherst Bulletin** (Mass.)*

Reading *La Presse* and *Le Devoir* these past few days, I wondered if before long M.L. wouldn't receive more sympathy than his victims, dead and wounded. "And the killer, he too was our son." writes Jacques Proulx. Nathalie Petrowski tells us: "I can't help it; for a week now I've thought of nothing but M.L."

Must we be reminded that M.L. very carefully, verbally and in writing, informed our society that the action he took was directed against feminists, whom he summarily defined as women having access to traditionally masculine professions? Whatever the past history and the state of mind of M.L., this man certainly intended that his act be interpreted as a political one. Yet many people question this. Have we ever questioned that Hitler was a politician because he was mad?

M.L.'s gesture was a complex act with personal, social, symbolic and political ramifications. Upon hearing about what he did, we responded individually, but also as a society. Yes, we cried over the death of his victims, each woman and each man privately weeping for the death of a sister, a friend, a daughter, a companion, a lover. But, as well, each woman cried over having been symbolically put to death. So it was that M.L.'s act of political terrorism entered into our private lives, precisely the way feminism had entered into the private life of M.L. Yes, the personal is political.

Alongside the personal loss experienced by a great number of us, we would do well to acknowledge that it was not just fourteen women who were mourned, but fourteen women students who were headed for promising careers. Socially, we felt the loss of a certain "investment." Just look at the list of associations, unions, and companies, including *le Conseil du patronat** and Hydro-Quebec, who expressed their sympathy. As for the Catholic church, the funerals of the victims gave the Church two good hours of free publicity.

On a political level, M.L.'s act was twofold: terrorist and targeted. To be sure, the terrorist act against women was condemned by the press, which required neither a great deal of analysis nor courage. The political act against feminists was something else, however. On this count, it was deemed preferable to fall back on M.L.'s madness, where a slight equivocation could let it be understood that feminists, in any case, tend to be excessive, that they are truly abominable to want to make something political out of the *demented* gesture of a *desperate* young man. So, gradually, we began to think it would make sense to let men be the first to speak in order that they might express how they were feeling and explain how feminism disrupts (irritates) their lives. Then petitions were organized against the sale of firearms, violence was spoken of as though it had never existed before the '80s—if it carries on like this, we'll be able to blame it on Meech Lake!** Anything to avoid showing solidarity with feminists and the feminist movement.

It is true that a certain exploitation of women is acknowledged, that too many women are beaten and raped but, at the same time, feminist analysis is not tolerated and nor is their deep reflection, their anger or their particular sadness. To show solidarity with feminists would mean admitting that feminists have not exaggerated the magnitude of men's contempt toward women, admitting they have not fabricated the day-to-day struggle inflicted upon women by men's domination, admitting that behind sexist discrimination, pornography, rape, and the systemic poverty of women are flesh-and-blood men—businessmen, men of law and religion. To show solidarity with feminists is to recognize that men have dug an unbelievable death trench with their misogynist lies, their phallocentric privilege,

* the largest employer group in Quebec
** site of a controversial federal-provincial meeting to amend Canada's constitution to include Quebec as a "distinct society."

and the "commonplace" intimidation that exists between women and men.

All things considered, M.L. was no young man. He was as old as all the sexist, misogynist proverbs, as old as all the Church fathers who ever doubted women had a soul. He was as old as all the legislators who ever forbade women the university, the right to vote, access to the public sphere. M.L. was as old as Man and his contempt for women.

As for the women who died, they were young, as young as the gains of feminism. They were even younger than they thought, much too young for a lone man armed with ancient mental equipment. They were as fresh as new life, which springs from the hope of each generation of women.

They Shoot Horses, Don't They?

This article appeared in La Presse on December 9, 1989.

Francine Pelletier

Horror and dismay. Whenever this American-style carnage happens, these same two words always spring to mind. "We don't understand why . . ." exclaimed the stunned director of the Polytechnique. "If we were in Medellin, we could say that it was political, ideological . . . but here . . ." mused the psychiatrist invited to the television program *Le Point.* "In twenty-five years, I've never seen such senseless killing," declared one police official.

Obviously, it is normal to be in a state of shock after such a massacre. When everything we take for granted in this society—the right to life, security, education—suddenly shudders and falls, we have every cause to feel seriously shaken. But we must stop thinking of these periodic eruptions of violence as strange anomalies, mysterious madness suddenly turned loose. In short, we must stop acting as though this violence has nothing to do with us.

Two "social" phenomena lie behind the murder of these fourteen women students. First, there is pathological homocide, which is becoming characteristic of North American society. It is widespread, and it spills a great deal of blood. In pathological homocide, the scenarios are consistently similar:

1) the killer has a pre-established plan;

2) he has every intention of being viewed as a Rambo-like figure in the public eye;

3) he bears a tremendous grudge against society, which continually flashes its power, wealth, and luxury but does not see fit to share any of it with him;

4) he kills innocent people, in front of television cameras where possible;

5) the killer is a man.

Behind this phenomenon, there is, to be sure, the fact that we glut ourselves with violence—through television, newspapers, sports—and we are interested in only the most spectacular entertainment, the greatest success. There is also the fact that men in our society are permitted, tacitly at least, to be violent.

But there is an even more serious phenomenon which explains the tragedy that befell us this week, and about this we speak very little. It is, of course, misogyny. A misogyny so precise and brutal that it brings to mind the witchhunts of earlier eras; a misogyny clearly expressed, lying right there in print, and yet we hasten to ignore it.

None of the persons interviewed last Wednesday night had an answer to the question: "But how can it be that *only* women were killed?" They all said, "This is what we don't understand."

And yet the answer is as clear as a mountain stream. A young man enters a classroom armed with a rifle, and evacuates the men from the room. To the women, he says: "You are all feminists. I hate feminists!" He kills some of them. He leaves, and moving from one floor of the building to another, he kills a few more as he goes. He kills himself in turn, leaving a message which says that women are hell, and that he would have liked to slay a few other particular women.

If this is madness, never has it been so lucid, so calculated. Never has madness taken such care to first identify and then eliminate the adversary. Never has madness left such a clear message. The message is: there is a
price for women's liberation and the price is death. Yes,
the killer was mentally ill and yes, this was a desperate
act, but killing fourteen women goes beyond "pathological homocide." It was an act of reprisal, well
thought out, calculated, and directed against women in
general and feminists in particular. It was an act of
reprisal which recalls a past we thought we would
never live again.

What this massacre tells us, in the end, is that we are
not quite the "evolved" society we thought we were.
And more particularly, it tells us that the re-negotiation
of the relations between men and women, begun
twenty years ago, is even more difficult than we could
have thought possible. Take, for example, this tidbit of
conversation overheard among three Radio-Canada
employees the day after the killing: one of the men
tossed off this remark, "Hey! He's not so bad, that guy.
I've often thought of doing that myself!"

A bad joke, of course, but one which says a lot about
the uneasiness that exists between men and women.
There has always been an uneasiness and there always
will be, because we are not "constituted" the same way.
But the discomfort goes beyond our biological differences, it goes beyond the fact that men have always been
apprehensive that women would snatch away "their
soul," and that women have always been afraid that
men would "beat up on them," physically or intellec-
tually.

There's something wrong here, and M.L.'s foul deed
shouts it from the rooftops. In my opinion, the malaise
is related to the way certain men (a minority, certainly,
but a minority that weighs heavy in the balance) interpret feminism. They regard feminism as a rejection of
men. It is not only that women today are able to take the
place of men—"take over" men's jobs, as they say. It is
much more a matter of women having a life of their
own, a matter of women not being available. And the
more women appear out of reach socially, the more they
appear unapproachable individually.

What is intolerable for some men today is that some women dare to be unavailable.

In 1984, for example, at *La Vie en rose,* * the magazine where I worked at the time, we had a bomb scare. Why? We were organizing for the second year in a row a March 8th celebration "for women only". The problem here was not that we wished to promote International Women's Day. The problem was that we had the nerve to do it without men.

Women don't have the right to ignore men—though men certainly have every right to ignore women. This is the message M.L. wanted us to remember.

If we are to go on the word of our elected representatives, women may be brutally attacked but they don't have the right to protection. Mr. Bourassa** spoke of the "tragedy" for the victims' parents. The new minister responsible for the Status of Women, Violette Trépanier, referred to the crime as an "isolated" case, and Mr. Parizeau*** spoke of "silence" as the only way to commemorate this tragedy. Not a single word about the fact that women are still completely vulnerable in our society!

Flags at half-mast? I'm all for it. But what difference does that make? It would be better to talk about control of firearms, the removal of violent programs from television, committees for the protection and promotion of women in public institutions. More important, men have got to stand up and say: Enough is enough! Slaughtering women is totally unacceptable.

The day men start saying that they too are afraid of this kind of behaviour, that it hurts them too, that they don't want any more of it—that's the day when things will start to change. Not before.

---

* *a well-known Quebec feminist magazine, published from 1980 to 1987*
** *Premier of Quebec*
*** *leader of the Parti québécois, a political party in Quebec*

Red Riding Hood

Nathalie Petrowski

This article appeared in Le Devoir on December 9, 1989.

I left the cinema. As chance would have it, on that fateful night of December 6 I had attended the premiere of *Bye Bye, Red Riding Hood,* the story of Little Red Riding Hood revised and set to rights by a feminist filmmaker. She'd had me shivering with fright at the sight of the big bad wolf circling about Little Red Riding Hood with his sickly smile, his fangs retracted. And then I sat back, reassured by the film that, at the end of this tumultuous decade, this treacherous symbol was impotent. The terrifying figure had disappeared, and in its place was a simple beast, a victim of its own demons.

Looking at his pathetic face, I was forced to recognize that the big bad wolf who had traumatized our childhood was no longer the powerful symbol he had once been. Under the postfeminist looking glass, he now appeared desperate, driven by a derisive need to possess what was beyond him and to swallow whatever he couldn't understand. For several minutes, I even felt a bit of sympathy for this wolf, who I knew would soon fall to the bullet of the good hunter hired to save the story. The moment was not long in coming. At sunset the hunter appeared on the screen and with one shot from a carbine rifle, the wolf was pulverized. The hunter then revived the grandmother and Little Red Riding Hood, and humanity could relax for a few hours.

Outside, it was as cold as if I was in Red Riding Hood's deserted forest. As I wondered if I shouldn't try to tame the big bad wolf myself, like the filmmaker had suggested at the end of the film, the first beads of the horrible tale began to be told one by one on the radio news, and there was nothing fairy-like about it. Not only did the big bad wolf still exist, he now had a real face, a cause, a rifle and a hunter's cap. And in his gaze, Red Riding Hood was no longer a lost little girl, but a young woman in a new generation that had decided to cross the forest alone, without suspecting that at the end of their sweat and tears there would be neither liberty, equality, nor emancipation. For them, there would be nothing but a pool of red blood.

Already, on the radio, dubious comparisons were being tossed off and achievement records compiled of the crazed killers who break and enter our lives armed to the teeth, with no target other than the society that produced them. The incident at the Polytechnique was third in importance and number, stated one commentator, as if there were some sort of national pride to be taken in this statistical account, as if now we would never again have to take a second seat to other societies, as if the unbearable violence of the last few hours somehow distinguished us as a community.

I then heard the fulminating question that was to come up again and again like an infernal litany. How can we explain that the gunman killed only women, the journalists were asking, like a bunch of children who don't understand how it can be that everything has been completely destroyed.

No one could explain it; no one understood it. Were they playing ostrich? Didn't they see that this gratuituous act was the offspring of a formidable logic gone mad? The crazed gunman of the Polytechnique was not so unusual. The sad precedent he had created was not related to the number of victims but to the fact that, for the first time in history—a history becoming more and more pathological—a gunman had calmly selected his victims.

Never in the course of this demented century has a mad gunman done this, and never in such a cold calculating manner. It's common knowledge that mad gunmen fire on anything that moves. They leave to professional psychopaths the grim task of singling out their prey and killing them one by one. Without knowing it, the mad gunman of the Polytechnique crossed the serial murder and the mass murder. How do we explain the fact that he chose the Polytechnique as the site of the crime, the journalists asked, wanting to fall back on chance (all they could think of to explain this barbaric lottery). But it was not by chance that the victims were enrolled at that ancient fortress of masculine hegemony, the Polytechnique. It was no coincidence that for the past several years women have invaded the school and in many cases, as one professor stated, they were just as competent, if not more so, than their male colleagues. It was not chance that, in the mad gunman's opinion, these women were out of line.

No, he wasn't crazy. His aim was accurate, straight to the heart of the highest symbolic site, the university, and especially the Polytechnique where, day after day, women calmly make their way through the worst kind of prejudice. With all the force of his misogyny and directed by his own internal rage he took straight aim, revealing much about himself and much about the society that witnessed his birth and watched him grow up in the forest. In his madness, he saw a war going on. And I ask myself today—as women's groups try to reinforce their positions by issuing press releases about violence against women, and journalists of the "stronger" sex shrug their shoulders, seeing in this act the isolated gesture of a guy who had come unhinged—I do ask myself if there really is a war, a war lurking beneath the surface.

Poor Little Red Riding Hood! Times have really changed. To think that she could have believed for even a moment that a good-hearted hunter would come to save her. But the hunter was afraid—he went away. As for the big bad wolf, he's running loose in the sheepfold, strong as ever, mad as ever, and nobody, not the psychologist, not the police, not the government, not the guy who sells arms, not society, seems able to stop him.

This letter appeared in Le
***Devoir** on December 9,*
1989.

Just for the Record

Denise Veilleux

Fourteen young women have just fallen to gunfire. This crime differs from other murders where an unknown individual aims haphazardly into the crowd. These victims were selected, separated from the mass of anonymous students for one reason and one reason only: they were women.

It certainly is a political crime, as one commentator put it, for it is a crime of sexism. Too often this term "sexism" has represented stereotyped attitudes ranging from paternalism to outright hostility, so much so that we associate it with symbolic or ideological confrontation.

The premeditated murder of the women students at the Polytechnique brings to the surface the crude reality of "the war of the sexes." Most women know one thing only too well: it's open season on women all year long!

Everyone is wondering what the murderer's motive could have been. The note he left shows that he deliberately chose women and, furthermore, that he didn't choose just any women students. He decided to slay young women destined for a profession still practiced mainly by men.

If this gesture is the act of a given individual, he was nonetheless following patriarchal society's common-law order: that women have no place in public life. Threats of violence, or recourse to violence, weigh heavily on all women who dare to step out of the narrow limits of the family home, the conjugal hearth and acceptable feminine roles.

The tragedy which has just taken place at the University of Montreal is a warning to all women, not only feminists. It is an official notice to stay in the background, and to leave to men their monopoly on knowledge, prestige, power and money.

Today, women everywhere are mourning the living strength of those young women so ruthlessly mowed down.

There will probably be some who point the finger at an indifferent or castrating mother, or at a frigid or wild girlfriend who "pushed" this young man to behave in this manner. Even in such an insane gesture we see the act of an individual driven by his own will.

Feminism has a strong back, doesn't it? And a good thing too, for it will likely be blamed for this *incident*, just as it was accused of having caused an increase in the incidence of rape.

Feminists have simply told the truth about these crimes, but society, in its false modesty, doesn't want to see the truth.

Far from lessening our resolve, the massacre at the University of Montreal reminds us that the battle is not yet won and reaffirms our determination to take our rightful place, indeed take everything that is rightfully ours, everywhere!

No More Excuses

Suzette Coulombe

This letter appeared in Le Devoir on January 19, 1990.

When the students were killed at the Polytechnique, I heard one of the survivors say, "We're only women..." Is it possible that today, in a supposedly evolved society, we still have to apologize for being women?

I'm not reacting against the person who said this, but against the M.L.'s who lie dormant in many men we know. And it is not a question of age, social class or training.

Why do students have so much trouble using "human being" instead of "man"? Why do my colleagues at work, with a barely-concealed smile, still make the same stupid remarks: "She's only a woman;" "Poor girl;" "It's no joke, being a woman."

Why does a man who is a union president oppose having a certain percentage of women on the union executive?

Why do men get upset when they see there are now three women labour leaders?

Why are men so merciless toward women who do the same jobs they do?

These are the same men who do not accept that they are sexist. They boast of their openness and their willingness to look at things critically. Yet we continue to see misogyny behind their words.

Does misogyny always come from men who are the products of a broken family and a difficult childhood? From men who are socially maladjusted because women are taking their rightful place in society?

Does it come from an obstinate refusal to recognize women as complete human beings?

Psychologists and psychiatrists seem to justify this behaviour by tracing it to education or the role of the father or mother. Sociologists blame it on a sick society, or a society in search of values. These excuses are too simple.

Is it not man himself who swells with pride because he is the most evolved, the most intelligent being on the planet? How can he keep a straight face, with all these massacres chalked up to his name? He is not even able to accept that women are different. That in 1990 we should still apologize for being women to these people with a virility hang-up, a predisposition toward guns, and a swelled head is absolutely revolting and unacceptable.

This catastrophe at the Polytechnique occurred at a politically opportune moment. Those of us who are men mustn't be afraid to admit this, and no, it is not paranoia on the part of us women; it is a warning for Quebec society. It is time to reflect on the relationships between men and women and to take action based on logic, not guns.

Murders and Misogyny

This letter appeared in Le Devoir on December 9, 1989.

Jean-Pierre Bibeau

I am not a psychiatrist and therefore would not know how to explain the destructive vision of the Polytechnique murderer, except for the fact that his underlying motives were clearly identified.

Two things demonstrate that the killer's mental illness was both the product of his individual psychological make-up and a social phenomenon. First, he chose as the site of his massacre a particular discipline: engineering. This was no coincidence. The killer did not go to the university to attack and kill a few people, then take his own life; he went to the Polytechnique, a carefully chosen site. The second characteristic of his murderous action was that he isolated the women from the men and ferociously attacked them. The women, not the men. Why the women? Because in his sick mind, this individual did not accept that women have access to courses in a technical discipline previously reserved for men. Maybe he truly did not accept that a woman could be something other than a body and a heart; that she could also be a brain.

"You are feminists!" he shouted, before destroying the brains that so disturbed him. Feminists because they wanted to build bridges, roads, dams. Because they dared to be present in a field of study reserved for men.

Yes, the massacre of December 6 is the product of a deranged mind. But this mind also planned who was to be killed. The killer set his sights on the women students because, as he said, "You have no business being here" (remark reported by a student on Radio-Canada that same night). The victims had been selected: women who were getting an education, and worse still, women who were studying to be engineers.

This misogyny was directly connected to insane destruction, as is too is often the case when women are murdered.

Unpublished letter, written on December 9, 1989 and submitted to Le Devoir.

A Matter of Life or Death

Élaine Audet

How to express how the heart is weighted down, the indescribable pain which seeps irreversibly into the skin of every woman who senses misogyny's malevolent weapon pointed straight at her life. Fourteen women, young, intelligent, full of dreams and the talent to make them happen, were coldly gunned down with the premeditation of three thousand years of woman-hating, reinforced by patriarchal societies built upon the domination of women and their children.

Wash your dirty linen at home, that's what the political and media representatives seem to be saying. Let the nice Quebec family lock itself away with its shame, and hide the fact that the son has gone out and ripped the life out of fourteen of his sisters who wanted only to be free. Play down the sexist, overtly anti-feminist motive of the crime. Yet if the killer had picked out a visible minority, everyone would have cried racism and remembered the Holocaust. Crimes against women have no history. This history, swept aside, wiped out, has only begun to be written. Hold back the anger which follows the pain, and instead let's talk about "the profound despair and rage which motivates a solitary insane killer, whose reasons for the crime we shall never know."

Every woman knows these reasons. They are transmitted to her at birth by the fathers, the brothers, the husbands who find it normal to subject her to their will and their desires. These reasons are quite obvious when a man wants to control a woman's body with force. They are obvious when, with the complete impunity of the family, the community, the media and the culture, a man believes himself justified to use women for his own purposes; to beat, attack, "incestuate," rape, and torture under the guise of fantasy; to clitoridectomize thousands of women in the name of tradition, as if we were groping in the darkness of the Middle Ages where you could do anything you wanted to the "sluts with no soul." How far will it go, our complicitous silence, even as we are faced with daily violence against women, in families, institutions, pornography, the media, advertising, cinema, and in literature where the sadistic misogyny of an author is attributed to his genius, to the grandeur of his symbolic universe, or to a sense of humour women seem unable to appreciate.

As more and more women refuse this age-old domination and take their rightful place in society, some men—so we hear—feel their identity is threatened. What kind of identity is this, if its existence is contingent on the non-existence of the Other? And furthermore, what kind of identity considers itself attacked as soon as a woman comes into her own as Subject, entering on the same footing a world which belongs to her as much as it does to those who colonised her mind and body in order to maintain her servitude and cut her off from her own desires?

How much longer will we try to cover up the selective nature of this crime, calling it violence in general, citing the availability of firearms, speaking primarily of individuals, people, students, victims, youth, cadavres, the dead, in order to keep our language from reflecting society's sexism? How much longer must we disguise the unbearable truth: this was the murder of fourteen innocent women and we must all assume responsibility by virtue of our silence, our complacency, our inertia.

As women, we will mourn our daughters, our sisters, our murdered friends, and we will carry the memory of them high. We will refuse the fear and intimidation this murderous act seeks to impose upon us, and we will fight to the very end for the liberty of each and every one of us.

A Matter of Life or Death: Second Installment

Élaine Audet

I can't help but think about the morning of Wednesday, December 6, 1989: young women getting out of bed as if it were any other day, appearing mildly distracted at breakfast, their heads full of details for the next exam, or vacation plans for Christmas. Dreaming. Thinking about life.

At that very moment, elsewhere in the city, someone who probably hasn't slept all night is writing his hate letter, preparing his weapon and his ammunition, going over each step leading him to his death mission. He's found scapegoats for his failures: women, who deny the existence of the old father who commands, gives orders, excludes, dominates, punishes, beats, who holds the right to life or death over women and their children. The killer-to-be knows that the Almighty father can never exist again, and he would do anything rather than accept the challenge his own life represents: to deserve, not overpower, the love which is no longer his privilege simply because he was born male. His reasoning is superficial, one-dimensional: women today are out of line; all feminists want to be like men, so there's only one solution, to put them in their place before it's too late, before men become human beings like everybody else. No more, no less.

For patriarchal man, what's critical is not the slow death of the planet caused by pollution, nor the threat of nuclear war, but the life that grows in the cracks of the exploitative system. This life derives meaning only from movement and renewal, the continuity that women carry within themselves from one generation to the next, and to which men, by nature, are not privy. Alienation from the reproductive cycle might explain their misogyny, forced as they are to recognize that all we know for certain, men and women, is that we are born of the belly of a woman and we go back to that of the Earth. This is unbearable certainty because it destroys thousands of years of false representation based on a delirious megalomania.

Even more disturbing is the knowledge that the patriarchy is neither eternal nor natural. It has an origin and therefore an end. Born of men's discovery of their role in procreation and their strength in appropriating women, children and the means of production (let us remember that it was women who invented agriculture), male power has never ceased to claim cultural grounds on which to base its "natural" right to invest the symbolic with its own values. The symbolic, this privileged means of apprehending and representing the unknown, was formerly the common property of men and women but now serves as the exclusive vehicle for patriarchal ideology and values. In this manner, the masculine-feminine opposition came to be insinuated in language, as was the domination of the feminine by the masculine, and ultimately the attribution of a negative or pejorative value to feminine symbols. Here lies the "yin" and the "yang" of all the theologies and philosophies men have invented to justify women's "inferiority" and camouflage their envy, fear and hatred of the female principle in nature.

The patriarchy, having begun at a certain time in history, is condemned to die. The day will come when sons will refuse a heredity based on senseless competition, violence and misogyny. The time is near when not a single woman will accept limitations on her aspirations and her desires by a sexual division of roles, the sole objective of which is to maintain the identity and the privileges of a supposed masculine supremacy. Destructive patriarchal history—the only one we know—is coming to an end in order that *human* history may begin.

The reassertion of patriarchal power taking place right now shows why women taking control over their own fertility and their lives is a critical political issue. By taking back our lives, we have the means to put an end to centuries of lies, contempt and injustice, and to deliver the final blow that will bring down the system of ownership which is the very foundation of all social, racial, and sexual divisions.

From a telephone poll of 1,000 Americans, conducted between October 23-25, 1989, the very conservative *Time* magazine obtained the following results: 95% of the respondents considered that the feminist movement helped women become more independent; 80% thought that it had given women more control over their lives; 82% stated that it continued to improve their condition; and 33% defined themselves as feminists (*Time*, December 4, 1989). Despite this encouraging data, we would be wrong to conclude that the era of postfeminism has arrived. The wage gap between men and women is still approximately 40% (Statistics Canada 1986); childcare services are insufficient; the incidence of rape is constantly on the rise; pornographic violence is growing by leaps and bounds; the double workday is a reality for the majority of women; abortion is a right which is constantly contested and threatened; contraception continues to be dangerous for women, etc.

Given the current state of feminism and the brutal reaction of the patriarchy to feminist gains, it becomes apparent that at the heart of feminist ethics lies responsibility. It is critical that we cease taking action solely as individuals, to the detriment of or without the knowledge of other women, giving rivalries and competition free rein among us. Men gave us this bone of contention to chew on, to keep us eternally divided and to allow themselves to remain the unique object around which our expectations and projects revolve. By each of our feminist acts we make a commitment to all women, promising to be of an exemplary nature and dedicated to self-esteem.

For women, being egotistical should be considered a positive quality, inasmuch as we've been accused of it ever since we claimed the right to determine our own lives. The patriarchy froze us in altruism, made us feel guilty if we dared to assert a capricious, original, joyous and liberated "I." The time has come to fill in the memory blank they've forced upon us; to fill it in with our Moons, our laughter, our shooting stars spinning with happiness, our light-filled and loving cleft which they try desperately to neglect and deride. It's more important than ever that we know, women and men, which side we're on—that of life or that of death.

We don't need to go looking for equality in the Church, the Army or the Management of large corporations. We don't have to plan for death, but rather take care of life, wherever it is mortally wounded by social inequalities, ecological disasters, genetic manipulations, cultural uniformity, overpopulation, the arms race, the ideologies of maximum profit and blind technological development, and wherever reproductive cycles are systematically ruined.

We don't want to plan for death. We're the ones who have always given life to the body of our imagination, to our sensual thoughts and to our overflowing hearts which quench that perfect thirst in the very deepest part of our memory. Happiness. Nothing less.

Bloody Quadrille

Louky Bersianik

As a woman conscious of living in a world still dominated by men, I refuse to endorse the power imbalance which allows patriarchal society to make decisions about my body, my desires and my needs, through laws which criminalize abortion or usurp my reproductive power with new technology. Above all, I refuse to consider the daily violence against women, in whatever form, a natural, isolated or commonplace phenomenon.

This violence throws itself in my path day after day and weighs heavily on my life and my writing. It makes me frustrated and angry, for it is the vulgar expression of a universal misogyny which permeates all cultures with its poison, made from a formula no one can decipher. What is unbearable is that this misogyny passes from one generation to the next in the form of knowledge, in works of art and literary masterpieces, in history, rituals and the customs of every country, since the beginning of time. This is a fierce misogyny, whose deleterious action takes place as much within religious, legal, medical, athletic and financial institutions as it does within the work world, families, the private life of each couple, and the organization of each social group. Upon this misogyny we have very little purchase, for it is not written under its real name in legal documents, good conscience and Christian doctrine. And even though it is not an aspect of human nature, it has become an inevitable and unavoidable aspect of the human condition in all eras and throughout all latitudes.

WHAT IS MISOGYNY? A monstrous parasite with an archaic cortex which has slowly worn away the human brain since the beginning of time. A violent emotion, it steers a course straight for the rape and murder of human females, all the while abusing them and using them as doormats or stepping stones.

Misogyny has nothing to do with an unhappy childhood, the absence of a father, too much or not enough love from the mother. It has nothing to do with the standard excuses that are always dredged up to exonerate men for their crimes against women. It has nothing to do with generalized violence.

Misogyny is a characteristic of civilization, a leftover barbarism that each generation believes it has definitively eliminated, but which reappears like ancient script on a palimpsest, at the slightest contrariness felt by any little backyard prince. Twenty-five centuries of hatred will not be ruled out by a simple initial at the bottom of a chart.

Misogyny is there when a child is born, when he or she grows up, gets married, dies. It is always there, latent or newly re-constituted, favouring boys and endangering girls. It accompanies the life of each human being, and fosters close ties with it, sometimes to the point of suffocation.

MISOGYNY IS HATRED, hatred pure and simple; hereditary hatred; irrational, illogical, murderous hatred.

Law courts resound with voices full of hatred and contempt for women, and it is from the judges' bench that these remarks emanate: " As we say, laws are like women, meant to be broken"; "It's no crime to beat your wife; it's chickenshit"; "The causes of conjugal violence can be traced back to the Department of Agriculture." And elsewhere, "Men have a right to beat their wives; women deserve it." One would believe that the judges are in agreement with the old Muslim proverb: "Beat your wife every day; if you do not know why, she will." For these men, this is not a simple sexist joke but an order heeded by all batterers.

Women too have had unhappy childhoods, they too have been sexually assaulted by a male parent (and much more often than their brothers), they too have been unloved children, they too have suffered due to the absence of their father or their mother. But we don't see women taking it out on men and little boys, subjecting them to all manner of atrocities, even murder; we don't see women arm themselves with a hunting rifle and only fire on men.

"I am a woman but I am not a human," says Euguélionne,* "for nothing is more human than to be inhuman." This violence directed toward the female of the species is specific to humans. Unless we renounce our humanity, all human beings must inevitably become conscious of the fact that misogyny is cultural and institutional, and that it insidiously affects the grey matter and the behaviour of each man and woman on this planet. I challenge the integrity of every patriarchal culture. In my eyes they've lost all credibility. I have no respect for them because ALL OF THEM are violent toward women, in a way which is not isolated, nor accidental, nor due to the odd mind afflicted with madness, but in a way which

* the title character of a novel by Louky Bersianik, published in 1976 and considered to be one of the most important feminist novels to come out of Quebec

encourages systemic and daily violence, physical and psychological violence.

I cannot consider myself human under a banner of violence. I am the object of hatred but I am not indifferent to hatred. Is it love that men want to destroy? When they themselves were nothing we gave our physical hospitality to these men who hate us enough to kill us. Every day we gave them bits and pieces of our body and soul so that, one day, they could be brought into the world. We protected them and they were suckled on our humanity and our love. You would think that they cannot bear the very best love, the least interfering love. They drag us, despite ourselves, into a macabre dance, one step forward, two steps back, and just before the last turn they throw us into the dungeon or the lion's den, and forget about us.

Societies which call themselves democratic must recognize in ordinary violence the root of evil eating away at them. They must examine the omnipresence of this particular violence aimed only at women, like the bullets of the killer at the University of Montreal last December. Throughout the centuries, in all eras and in all social milieu, we witness this *bloody quadrille* which separates human beings into two categories, whether they are white, black, Jewish, Christian, Arabic, Muslim, whether they live in modest conditions or in wealth: WOMEN ON ONE SIDE, MEN ON THE OTHER, so that, among the human beings present, there will be no mistake about who can be massacred, wiped out, mutilated, beaten to death, or reduced to nothingness with impunity.

The greatest violence that can be inflicted upon a group is to deny the existence of violence, and to make the group's reaction the "real" problem. In other words, to frame their protest as the real violence. For example: "Let's not talk about violence against women; let's talk about how women are violent!" Or: the victim inflicts violence upon the killer, for she makes him do her a big favour. The power of the victim, know what I mean?

It is common knowledge that the most effective way for the oppressor to justify himself is to place blame on the person he oppresses. This phenomenon has been apparent for a very long time in the courts: it's the fault of the victim if she allows herself to be beaten, raped, harassed or sexually assaulted. This is Freudian discourse *par excellence* with regard to women, turning the facts around, distorting reality. In incest cases, it is little girls who do the seducing, mothers who are to blame for it. This discourse coincides perfectly with that of the bible: Eve committed Adam's sin.

At the end of her book *La Porte du fond*, Christiane Rochefort quotes Françoise Dolto: "In father-daughter incest, the daughter adores her father and is very pleased to be able to thumb her nose at her mother! QUESTION—So, the little girl is always consenting? DOLTO—Precisely. QUESTION—But after all, there are plenty of cases of rape, no? DOLTO—There is no rape at all. They consent to it."

And Rochefort, in the body of the text, writes: "And who would believe you? People don't believe children. Guard dogs, always on duty, will continue to bark at kids caught in the parental trap, 'They all consent to it.' That's what kills me; that's the coup de grâce." Freud and his unconditional followers are the spokesmen for the patriarchy, and the judges base themselves on Freud and the Bible, in order to condone violence against women and girls. Recently, newspapers reported a case of incest involving a little girl three years of age. The judge declared that this little girl had contributed to the incest because she had been sexually aggressive! Clearly, fathers need protection from their little girls. What next? An ombudsman for men who are sexually assaulted by their children?

We could well ask why men continue to hound us when they have all the power, when the world was made for them and by them, and when this world continues to function à la masculine? Why do they still need to crush us with violence, why do they always have to put us "in our place" by force, when contempt alone is not enough? Why are judges misogynists and full of prejudice toward women? Why is the man who murders his wife, the father who rapes his daughter, considered mentally ill and not a criminal?

There are men who are starting to be clairvoyant and who dare to speak out: "All men are guilty," writes Dorval Brunelle, professor and sociologist at the University of Quebec in Montreal. "Feminists have every reason to rise up; all these crimes are political, and the latest, the one at the Polytechnique, is supremely so. The affidavit is clear and proof is at hand: in the present state of affairs, men are incapable of establishing equality between the sexes. What they give with one hand, in charters or laws, they swiftly take away with the other, when they desecrate certain values and destroy lives."*

"In masculine fantasies," says Robbe-Grillet, "woman's body is the ideal site for the crime." Only in fantasies? Well, thank you, good apostle! Fantasies like this selective mass murder at the Polytechnique (winter 1989), like this odious injunction against the body of Chantal Daigle** (summer 1989), like this gang rape at

---

* *Le Devoir, December 12, 1989*
** *Chantal Daigle was restrained by a court injunction from having an abortion*

McGill University (1988), like the murder of Hélène Lizotte by her husband (August 1987)?! Fantasies like the women who are battered every day; like the women murdered by the Love of their Life; like the women raped, tortured, burned alive for not having a dowry; like the women who are for sale, prostituted?! Fantasies like the little girls forced into incest, pornographied, clitoridectomized, murdered, infibulated, assassinated, dismembered, cut into pieces, thrown out with the garbage! Miscellaneous fantasies such as those worthy of publication in *Allô Police*! "Leave our fantasies alone," bawl the Robbe-Grillets of freedom of speech, "They don't hurt anyone."!!!

Our democracies are so hypocritical, they would take the breath away from each and every one of us. ENOUGH IS ENOUGH!

FEARFUL WORDS

This letter appeared in **Voir** *on December 14 and in* **La Presse** *on December 20, 1989.*

Letter to the Media

Louise Malette

Fourteen women have just been killed because they were women. Sad, but true. The trouble the media has taken to dismiss this undeniable fact absolutely horrifies me.

To speak of the murderer using his first name almost affectionately, as if he were our little brother, is so absurd it makes me shudder.

The great care taken to ensure that men, particularly those who witnessed the tragedy, are not blamed for anything, instead of being concerned about the terror experienced by the real victims—the young women who were wounded, and all those who happened to escape the massacre—is enough to make one's hair stand on end. Someone actually managed to extract words of pity for the attacker from the very mouth of one of the victims on her stretcher. It's like an hallucination!

It is vile that the newspaper stories revolve around the murderer and his favourite kind of jam. Fortunately for us he's dead—if he weren't, we would probably be graced with his presence on all the TV talk shows. You have only to read *Le Devoir* to believe it! It devoted its Saturday edition to the murderer's emotional problems—poor little guy!—when he's just killed fourteen women, wounded another thirteen, traumatized for life a good hundred, and awakened in all the rest anguish and dread. This is indicative of extremely poor taste. Furthermore, it indicates a lack of professional integrity that can mean only one thing—cowardice. That *La Presse*, for its part, divulged the names and photos of women who were listed in the notorious letter the killer carried on his person is proof of a disconcerting lack of professional ethics. (Just for the record, we note that prior to tossing the hit list to the journalists' den, the police removed the names of six or seven policewomen listed in the original!)

When I think of that poor young girl who, lying on her stretcher, said that she wasn't even a feminist, I feel like crying. When I think of that girl in the classroom, the only one who tried to reason with the killer, crying out: "We're not feminists. We're only women who want an education," I feel like screaming. She did not understand that this is exactly what she shouldn't have said. Maybe a different approach would have done the trick: "No, no. Don't shoot. We're only human beings who want an education." Too bold. Instead: "No, you see .. . we're not really human beings . . . just things . . . nothing, really . . . we are nothing, nothing at all. Please. Have pity, don't shoot . . . please, sir . . . "

Feminists have never had good media coverage. In the years when feminism was really a hot topic, the media didn't miss a chance to denigrate the feminist struggle and show their contempt for it. We have never benefited from the direct support of the media, and those women who did not hide their sympathy for the feminist movement paid for it with their jobs.

By denying the sexist nature of these killings and, consequently, preventing feminist analysis from illuminating the social and political ramifications of this event, the media has lost a good occasion to exonerate itself. By failing to look truth in the eye, journalists in the pay of the media (and therefore in the pay of an ideology) contribute to contempt, hatred, and violence toward women which, this time, took the form of insanity. This zeal to undermine the obvious and distract public attention from the real questions is called, I think, manipulation. In this instance, it is an expression of fear which, if measured by its effect, must be still greater than the collective fear of women it deliberately tries to muffle.

This letter appeared in La Presse on December 20, 1989

Enough is Enough

Gisèle Gaudreault and Louise Mignault

(to Roger D. Landry, *La Presse*)*

We are writing to express our disapproval of the way some of your journalists reported the tragic events of the sixth of December.

Is satisfying the morbid curiosity of your readers sufficient reason to add to the distress of Madam Monique Lépine by laying before the general public details of her private life, which are no one's business?

Might we be trying to blame her for this tragedy and does that explain our behavior? The journalist's job is to inform people, not to encourage collective voyeurism.

Madam Lépine herself is a victim of her son's aberrant behaviour, and is therefore deserving of our sympathetic concern.

Excerpt from a special edition of the McGill Daily-Link, produced by women students at McGill and Concordia Universities, and the University of Quebec, December 7, 1989.

Dying to be a Woman

Josette Côté,
President,
National Assocation of Quebec Students

An unfortunate and isolated act! Why not a "natural disaster," while we're at it? We're trying to cover things up with phrases like, "It's sad, and that's all there is to it." What should we do? Wait for another mass murder? How many "isolated acts" like this are chalked up to society? Say, Mr. Bourassa,** aren't there already

* *editor-in-chief of that newspaper*
** *see note page 36*

enough women killed, beaten, raped, harassed? "Oh, come on . . . that's life," seems to be the best answer we can come up with.

No. Violence against women is not *"life."* It is not a normal phenomenon, part of the ups and downs of our society. It is a reality we can work on at the social level, and it is in this sense that feminists work for change. Women organize for equality, and for a life without fear and loathing. I am one of those "creatures" society considers strange, marginal and threatening: a feminist. I am one of those women who is in mourning because we are women. I am one of those women who wonders when the day will come when women won't have to live in fear.

Men Hogging the Mike Again!?!

Martin Dufresne, for the Men's Collective Against Sexism

This letter appeared in Le Devoir on December 7, 1989 and January 28, 1990.

Just last night I was at the march organized by the Women's Collective of Concordia University and the Committee for the Defense of Women in Montreal. I would like to comment on the manner in which certain male student leaders did everything they could to prevent the women organizers of this event from speaking to the crowd. I understand and share what both the men and women students felt, but to impose silence or prayer is not the only way to validate, and to recover from, the experience of horror—one must also understand, speak out, react, protest. The antifeminism of the killer is strangely echoed by those who would again censor women, by preventing them from saying what everybody knows perfectly well: it was misogyny that struck Wednesday, not an "incomprehensible act."

Had it been a white man in a racially-mixed school who had chosen to kill only blacks, would we have hesitated for a single second to call this a racist act? Would we have had the impudence to prevent the black community from protesting? Women's groups assembled everywhere in Canada last night. Only in Montreal were women prevented from taking the mike.

The women and men who were part of the much-vaunted "spontaneous procession to the Oratory" experienced this silencing phenomenon in a different context. Student leaders at the Polytechnique, having ceased all their usual student activities, had unilaterally decided to walk toward St-Joseph's Oratory under an imposed silence. Thousands of men and women responded when the organizers put the word out. We watched as women were harassed, insulted and deprived by force of their modest sound equipment. They decided not to fight, no doubt to avoid yet another flare-up of sexist violence. And the media had the image they wanted. Silence is golden, is it not?

Was it simply a spontaneous decision? No more than the religion of our childhood, with all its ramifications in our current laws and lives.

Burying Women's Words:
An Analysis of Media Attitudes

Armande Saint-Jean

A lot of things were said about what happened at the Polytechnique, and a lot of things were left unsaid. Overstatement and a shortage of ideas: the two poles of the paradox.

When Quebec journalists got together a few weeks after the event to examine their consciences, some congratulated themselves for having done a good job when the killings took place last December. They congratulated themselves for fast reflexes, intensive coverage, and the balance they achieved between curiosity and respect for the victims. Only a few voices surfaced against the current, a few discordant notes floating about in the sea of congratulations. Had the media truly projected an accurate portrait? As Ariane Émond* put it, were the journalists concerned about conveying the "great collective pain" of the women of Quebec?

On the night of December six, I was working. At the journalism workshop at the University of Quebec at Montreal, I was helping a group of thirty journalism students produce our daily paper for the next day. This workshop of students who were learning how to write and edit became my microcosm for observing the reactions we journalists have in such circumstances.

In the beginning the dispatches were confused: a wild gunman had fired on people at the Polytechnique. Who had been hit? Were there any dead? How many wounded? It was only as the hours went by, and as news bulletins and special reports were broadcast live on the radio and television that we managed to piece together the complete picture. In the end, twenty or twenty-one hours had passed before we could be absolutely *certain* that the victims were ALL women.

Why was this so hard for them to say? Why, from the very first moments, had it been so difficult, so awkward, for them to articulate the reality of the situation. Women, only women had been killed. Strange, though *victime* is a word which has only one gender in French—the feminine. Why was the incident immediately

* *Quebec feminist and journalist*

labelled "inexplicable," "incomprehensible"? Why was Lépine immediately classified as a "raving madman," as if that would explain everything?

All evidence shows that this man committed an insane act. But he did it in a lucid, conscious manner. He suffered a sort of madness, certainly, but not the kind of insanity that severs all contact with reality and plunges one's conscious mind into total unconsciousness. His gesture was completely thought out, consciously chosen, premeditated: he even took the trouble to explain it in a letter he wrote. The murderer himself furnished all the evidence necessary to understand what he'd done.

The first violent, intolerable misogyny came to me over the radio. An open-line program allowed listeners to express their off-the-cuff reactions all night long. There were few women callers, and some of the more disgusting reactions began showing through. Unsavoury individuals, clotted with bitterness and rancour, began to spit up what others had no doubt thought, but wouldn't say.

The killer (who was totally ignored at this point) was thought to have done something despicable, but he had nevertheless exhibited some of the anger men feel toward these women today who display an "exaggerated feminism." He knew that his future was compromised: these days, with abortion, divorce, independence, there's no way to find a good little wife to bear your children anymore. Such frustration is bound to explode in the light of day, they said to themselves, so we needn't be surprised!

I was completely shattered, heart-broken, overwhelmed. The next day I would run across them, those men, on the street, at work, in the subway. They wouldn't dare say another word, but I would feel the hatred coming from them, the way humidity penetrates to the bone in winter. They wouldn't dare hit me, I knew, but their look would communicate that hatred and violence.

And of course, the next day, nothing. A thick veil of shame seemed to have been deposited on our little land, like a sea of fog. A heavy clumsy shame you could cut with a knife. The women were suffering and did not know how to look at the men, including "their" man. The men didn't know what to do, what to say, or how to say it. Awful. We have never felt further apart.

Everyone cried. And in this immense national pain where words failed to express the tragedy, the media played the role of official mourner—something they know how to do so well when called upon. We were treated to journalism reserved for great occasions: front-page colour photos, huge screaming headlines, pages full of personal stories, photos from family photo albums. We read everything, watched everything, listened to everything. But we were still hungry, for all this material eventually wearied us, without ever satisfying us.

Desperate, we repeated the inevitable "why?", we played out the astonishment, feigned total incomprehension. We also directed our conscious attention—and this is still going on—to the examination of the personal life of Marc Lépine, as if it would offer more clues than society, encased in its splendidly triumphant misogyny, could offer.

Oh, and then the gurus arrived. They were everywhere at once: on radio, on TV, in the Saturday edition of daily papers. Our designated wise men were being asked to explain the incident, name the punishment, show us how to reflect upon this. I read the published analyses and editorials. I listened to Pierre Bourgault's sermon on Radio-Canada. I agreed in part, disagreed with the rest, but what difference did it make! Most of all, I was angry: Pierre Bourgault, like the others, only said what feminists have been saying for twenty years. Why was he asked, why were *they* asked to say this?

Here were a good crop of psychologists, sociologists, *men*-ologists. Here were a bunch of "good" guys, for the most part, who have learned to think differently from their older brothers, and who concluded by endorsing the fundamental points that we women have put forward and defended for years. It was our national gurus, the Chabots, the Brunelles, and Champagne and company, that the media wanted to see consoling the distraught population. Them, and only them.

Why were *men* asked to cast light on all this? The fact that they were often *progressive* or pro-feminist doesn't change anything. Why was it not considered advisable to ask *women* to give their reading of events?

Several women, whose commentaries are usually sought after, brought to my attention that *no one* had contacted them in the days following the killing. Why?

I began to understand the reason when I was invited to speak on a CBC radio program* and heard a journalist colleague accuse *certain pressure groups* of having taken advantage of this tragedy to advance their cause!

---

* *One day we'll have to ask ourselves why it was that the English press covered the massacre so much better than the French press. Everyone seems to agree this was the case. Was it because they were less directly involved? Would things have been the same if the tragedy had occurred in an English community, at Concordia University or at McGill, and if the killer had an English-sounding name?*

What were they talking about? Feminists? How could they dare say such a thing? It was grotesque. Not to mention that hardly any women's voices were heard addressing the issue. And when they did . . . well, the remarks of the Minister Responsible for the Status of Women were rather ambiguous, when we had hoped for something more direct, more powerful.

I came to understand that, actually, the words of women were not wanted. The explanations we would give, our visions of reality, were unbearable. We were not supposed to show—particularly with facts at our disposal—that this was a killing which reproduced on a larger scale a tragedy which many women, which *all* women live on a daily basis.

Very early on, sharp directives fell down all around us. We were above all not to say that in every male a Marc Lépine could be found lying dormant. We were also not to say that the fourteen women students at the Polytechnique were, in fact, symbols; that they embodied the progress women have made in the past two or three decades, by inhabiting spheres that men have kept for themselves ever since the beginning of time.

Above all we were not to tell the truth, nor cite the evidence. Why? Because of the bad conscience of those who still benefit from a system of oppression which feminists condemn, and which hasn't disappeared, regardless of what we say about it.

Reality is cruel. Not only the reality of this incident at the Polytechnique, but the reality of the daily lives of women—and men—who remain imprisoned within modern patriarchy. And this reality is as difficult to unmask as the glaring injustices of ten or twenty years ago.

The media has often indulged in the mouthwash of *postfeminism*. This serves primarily to convince them that changes which have taken place are largely sufficient, and that feminism ought to be regarded as an outdated ideology. They have also taken pains to present the generation of younger women as non-feminists.

It is no doubt comforting to note that those women who are twenty year olds today believe they have come into a world which doesn't look anything like the one their mothers lived through. Wait a minute! Yes, some things have changed in a fundamental and irreversible way. But we are still a long way from having reformed the system which confers on males, from the moment they are born, a status which is superior to that of girls and women.

The media has been devoid of feminist discourse for a good ten years now. We *tolerated* it for a period of time—but *tolerance* has its limits, does it not? The media, so quick to seize a society's new fads and trends, were not very accommodating in the long run. The world of newscasting, like many others, remains permeated with a conservatism it calls respectability.

Over time, feminists understood that they would not be tolerated anymore, that no one was interested in hearing from them anymore. And they learned to modulate their discourse, to make themselves less threatening, above all not to be aggressive—in short, to go back to their groups, their activities. We learned how to break down walls long before we spoke up about it in public.

Too bad. We could have made an important impact if we had been able, from the morning after the Polytechnique killing, to break into public consciousness and explain that this act represented nothing less than *systematic* violence against all women. Women should have been able to specify that the control of firearms, semi-automatic or otherwise, will not in itself take care of the problem, and neither will the abolition (however desirable) of violent films on TV or at the cinema.

Women should have been able to express the terrible horror we feel because of the death of these young women, and also the horror we feel for the fate of all women subjected to attack, rape, physical abuse, and harassment. The media plays the role of the weeping women of ancient times. But nowhere does society agree to let women cry over their own fate. Nowhere do they let us cry out, protest or simply talk about it. The only ones who are allowed to speak are those who echo the system's dogma, those who think they're somebody, those who think they're like men.

We should have been able to say that of all the kinds of horror we feel about the Polytechnique tragedy, what disturbs us most is the resulting intimidation of all women, especially the younger ones.

We should have been able to get a message of hope and solidarity out, loud and clear, despite our sadness, to all those who fight to change things.

We should have been able to pass along this rallying cry: "No! We will not be intimidated!"

Instead, we were treated to a first class burial. The words of women were covered over once more.

This letter was published in Le Devoir on January 8, 1990.

We Don't Understand

Mireille Brais

The media and their talk show hosts, surrounded by psychologists and psychiatrists, tried desperately to wrap their heads around the event. "We don't understand what happened," they cried, when clearly they should have listened to their hearts. The images were there; the words the killer used and the letter he wrote couldn't have been more clear.

Similarly, we cannot understand how an honest citizen, a man who goes to work, wears a suit and has a family, a man without a criminal record and a man who has not robbed a bank or imported drugs, could come to the point where he would kill his wife.

Our lack of understanding is such that we persist in using the label "a crime of passion" to categorize what amounts to a man killing his family and then committing suicide. We don't understand that a man could rape women and children.

The more specific and concrete the act, the less we understand it.

We understand, on the other hand, that a man is paid more than a woman. We understand that a man, who has reached the limits of his patience, could hit his wife a few times. We understand that a man could rape a woman who accepted to have dinner with him, and even let herself be driven back home later.

We understand pornography and beer ads. We understand that they could want to "fix" all those bloody feminists.

But with a look of total confusion, we absolutely do not understand the killing that took place at the Polytechnique. We don't understand, because if we were to understand, we would know that the man who pulled that trigger was not alone.

The Art of Making it Work for You

Andrée Côté

On December six, fourteen women students were killed by Marc Lépine for the simple reason that they were women who had stepped out of line. Because this happened, the women students at the Polytechnique were identified as feminists. "The Polytechnique is itself a symbol of the greatest advances made by women who enter non-traditional fields."[1]

If we are to go by the assertions of certain people, men experience the advent of women into their territory as a violation, a "penetration." "Women are taking up more and more space . . . some men feel threatened."[2] They "don't know where to turn or what to do,"[3] their "values are in a state of collapse,"[4] and many submit to the "feminist revolution" with "rancour."[5] Why be surprised then if some of them attempt to make women toe the line? Why be surprised if some men want to put women in their place, at home with the children, the elderly, and the misfits?

Marc Lépine, however, went further than Jean-Guy Tremblay. Lépine committed a previously-unimaginable crime: he massacred a group of women. From this time on, we will be haunted by this act. The seriousness of Marc Lépine's crime is directly proportional to the extent to which its significance has been eclipsed, rendering men's violence toward women once more invisible. To accomplish this, the news media ignored feminist expertise on male violence, and made room instead for psychological discourse.

At the outset, Marc Lépine was designated as a "sick man,"[6] a "mad killer,"[7] a "maniac."[8] Having characterized him in this way, one could dismantle the political impact of his crime: "This is not a social phenomenon, but an individual gesture carried out by someone who was sick."[9]

It is no coincidence that the same terms are often used to describe both the men who beat their wives and the men who kill their wives. The concept of mental anomaly is now paradigmatic, not only when it is a matter of domestic violence,[10] but also in cases of incest, rape and, to a certain extent, pornography and prostitution. The real nature of crimes against women is camouflaged, and the attackers appear to be the victims.

After having relieved Marc Lépine of responsibility for his actions, certain psychologists were able to dole out the benefit to all men: "No one can be accused of cowardice in this tragedy."[11] "It would be unjustified and unfortunate to accuse boys of not having been courageous."[12] Nothing was spared, in order that men not become the victims of "guilt feelings."[13] Then the psychologists turned their attention to the women survivors and their families. And what was the interpretation they offered these people? They reiterated that "This tragedy shows that we live in a non-violent society,"[14] and that these women need not be worried, for "mass murder remains a singular phenomenon."[15] We know that the psychologists brought relief to the survivors, but what was the truth backing up their point of view?

The psychologists were not the only ones to let the massacre of fourteen women students work to their advantage. The Catholic church benefited enormously from the event. The priests gave of themselves to their heart's content, openly revelling in their ecclesiastical travesty. Cardinal Paul-Émile Léger went so far as to state that the death of these women must be seen as "an offering made to God."[16] The only commentator who publicly denounced the hypocrisy of this "sexist" and "misogynist" Church, and who dared say to the priests, "Keep quiet, you! Get out of the way, and let a woman speak,"[17] was fired.

Men in positions of power did not want to admit that this crime represents a crime against women. Premier Bourassa hastily asserted that the event had no political significance: unlike the murders committed by members of the F.L.Q.* "it was not a matter of deliberate acts of political violence,"[18] he stated.

Although our statesmen are inclined, at election time, to make speeches filled with rhetoric about official equality, they refuse to admit that the subordination of women by men is the social substratum upon which the present system rests. The current policies of the federal and provincial governments show us that Marc Lépine and Jean-Guy Tremblay** are not the only ones to want to put women in their place.

The Mulroney government in particular wants to control women with its abortion law: this law is as important on a symbolic level—the defeat of the feminist movement—as on the practical level. In fact, it provides the State with an efficient tool to actualize control over maternity. The Bourassa government also wants to

---

*   *Front de la libération du Québec, a revolutionary movement promoting the emergence of an independent, socialist Quebec*

** *Tremblay had a court injunction brought against his former companion, Chantal Daigle, because she wanted to procure an abortion. The case was brought to the Supreme Court of Canada, who decided in favour of Daigle*

send women back to their pots and pans, thanks to its new family policy, which upholds a philosophy called "welcoming life."[19] This policy plans to put into effect a "regulatory program" which would register women faced with an unwanted pregnancy. Adoption is pushed as the alternative solution to abortion, and "psychological" support is envisioned for the woman who does not want to carry her pregnancy to term. As well, the government is committing itself to generously subsidize men's groups for male batterers and organizations which "promote the family."

After the massacre of these women students Mr. Mulroney had the nerve to want to calm our rage with a pornography bill—this, when we we had already learned that his government generously subsidized the pornography industry.[20]

The final report we will draw up for this "postfeminist" decade is sombre. Women have been the victims of serious attacks on the part of the State, such as the salary cuts endured by women public servants, economic losses suffered by divorced women, and the increasing number of men awarded custody of children. Free trade, and the proposed changes to the Unemployment Insurance Act, have us anticipating the even greater impoverishment of women. Incest, rape and sexual harassment are still very difficult to prove in court. Pornography is a little less visible than it was, perched on shelves four or five feet off the ground and discreetly packaged, but the message has not changed.

Fourteen women are dead simply because they were women. How can we accord our politicians any credibility now, if they refuse to acknowledge the manifestation of the most blatant misogyny Quebec has ever known?

> *Text of a speech delivered December 13, 1989 at l'**Union française**, at a gathering organized by women's groups on the theme of "Countering political crimes against women and lesbians."*

Notes

1. Micheline Bouchard, 1969 Polytechnique graduate, *La Presse*, December 9, 1989

2. M. Landreville, Director, School of Forensic Sciences, University of Montreal, *La Presse*, December 9, 1989

3. Mario Fontaine, journalist, *La Presse*, December 9, 1989

4. Jean-Paul Desbiens, *La Presse*, December 9, 1989

5. Maurice Champagne, *La Presse*, December 9, 1989

6. Thérèse Daviau, *La Presse*, December 8, 1989

7. "Maryse Leclair's mother feels only pity for the crazed killer." *La Presse*, December 8, 1989

8. "Diane Gamache can't believe that she's still alive: the maniac missed her two times." *La Presse*, December 8, 1989

9. Dr. Yves Lamontagne, *La Presse*, December 8, 1989

10. By way of example, let us recall that Judge Henri-Rosaire Desbiens asserted that domestic violence is a "psycho-social"problem, at the When Love Hurts conference, held in Montreal April 13 and 14, 1989 (Proceedings published by Éditions Saint-Martin)

11. Dr. Yves Lamontagne, *La Presse*, December 8, 1989

12. Pierre Achille, Director, Psychology Department, University of Montreal, *La Presse*, December 8, 1989

13. Lyne d'Amours, of the Corporation of Psychologists

14. Pierre Achille, *La Presse*, December 8, 1989

15. Dr. Yves Lamontagne, *La Presse*, December 8, 1989

16. Cardinal Paul-Émile Léger, December 8, 1989, CKAC Radio

17. Pierre Bourgault, *Ici comme ailleurs*, Radio-Canada, radio section, December 13, 1989

18. Robert Bourassa, interviewed by Bernard Derome in the context of a special program on Radio-Canada (television section) on December 7, 1989

19. "Families First, Family Action Policy Plan 1989-1991," sponsored by the Secretary of State for the Family, the Government of Quebec, 1989

20. Allusion to the thousands of dollars that the Federal Business Development Bank loaned to certain "topless" bars in the Hull area

When Cracks Appear in the Varnish

Marie-Thérèse Bournival

I don't want to make a big deal out of this and, in my rankling bitterness, throw out the other fifty percent, but there are some acts which fill one with more than horror.

There are some acts which make a society shed the coat of varnish which its political parties, struggling with diehard unrelenting feminists, once did their best to paint on. I've often heard it said that the women of Quebec are respected and admired by women elsewhere, and this has always consoled and encouraged me.

But following such brief moments of optimism, I interview nurses treated like servants, women brutally beaten in the stomach (preferably after a cesarian), children under twelve years of age who have to give in to the sexual demands of their father, their stepfather, or the boys in their class.

The inequalities are old, but the women of Quebec are young.

Sixty years ago, the first woman was admitted to the Senate. Until then, women were not considered "persons" in the legal sense, and were refused admittance to the Senate by the British North America Act.

Forty-eight years ago women finally managed to register for courses in law, after overcoming twenty-six years of resistance.

A mere forty-four years ago, *Le Devoir* made public a speech by barrister Perreault, who did not suppress his eagerness for women to finally acquire full judicial rights—rights recognized for everyone domiciled in Quebec except "those who were not fit," that is, children who were not of age, people who were insane and married women.

Thirty years ago, school boards forced women teachers who became engaged to leave their teaching positions. In this way, it was thought that there would be nothing stopping these teachers from "having their families." Find the mistake in this picture.

The mistake could be this varnish—the varnish of acquired rights when the wood is still too green and not aged enough for the translucent coating of laws and social policies.

The mistake may be that the train of legal recognition and equal opportunity programs, though it came in at a snail's pace, still entered the station too quickly for the enormous load of prejudices transmitted from generation to generation. Yes, we have advanced in many areas. Yes, our legislation, especially that of the last fifteen years, is some of the most progressive there is. So what?

The electronic counter was set back to zero one night in December. Rifle shots brought back our memory—the memory of our youth when the issue was women's rights in Quebec. Rifle shots forced us to critically examine our choice of society.

As Claire Bonenfant* emphasized during a recent interview, we only have to look at the universal social programs that are slowly and progressively being withdrawn. These programs are extremely important to women. There is the new automobile insurance law which offers absolutely no protection for the woman who has decided not to work out of the home. And the social welfare law where a pair of pants hanging behind a door is taken as evidence that a woman has a boyfriend who's a leech. There's the actual situation in the community colleges where, out of forty-six colleges, not one president is a woman.

Not to mention this game of the one hand not knowing what the other hand is doing: on one hand, acknowledging women's expertise when it comes to, for instance, shelters for battered women, and youth homes; and on the other hand, policies that cut the funds for such establishments. And let's not forget this game of musical chairs, where the "experts" are invited to come and talk about what happened at the Polytechnique. I saw Bernard, Yves . . .

You don't have to scratch very hard—it's a thin coat. Yes, it's cracking, and not just at the Polytechnique.

*   *past president of the Advisory Council on the Status of Women*

The Common Assassination of Women

Mireille Trudeau

This letter, written December 14, 1989 and sent to Le Devoir and La Presse, went unpublished.

Following the mass murder of fourteen women at the Polytechnique there was a rapid multiplication of media coverage, indignant reactions and messages of condolence from various institutions and professional associations.

Many of these messages made reference to "students cut down in the flower of their life" (Claude Ryan, December 6), "wounded students and witnesses," "employees and professors" of the institution, "friends" of the victims (Hydro-Quebec, December 8 and the University of Quebec in Montreal, December 8).

It is surprising and deplorable to note that only the masculine gender has been used, when the French language, conservative though it may be, has access to the following: *étudiante, employée, amie* and, more recently, *professeure* (Office de la langue française).

This stubborn erasing of the feminine gender is disturbing when we know that it was a matter of thirteen *étudiantes* "cut down in the flower of their life," an *employée* of the Polytechnique and nine wounded *étudiantes;* that there were other women students there, who were probably more terrorized than their male colleagues and in greater need of condolences. Once more it is a matter of *mères* and *pères*, of *amies* described as *amis*. This exclusion of the feminine at such a moment is significant. How to not read this as the obstinate refusal to recognize female reality, to name it as such and, more important, to acknowledge its right to exist?

By not specifically denominating those who were singled out we deny the existence of the people whose assassination we lament. Does this not doubly annihilate them?

Since the French language has only two genders and not a third universal or neutral one (with which to offer condolences to students, professors, employees and friends) to avoid mentioning women students, women professors, women employees, and women friends who were devastated, is to collaborate in the common assassination of women.

Words and Deeds

Sylvie Bérard

I am writing to try to alter the destiny of fourteen women, in order to change a tiny bit of the lives of 3 million Québécoises, of 2.5 billion Earthlings, of 52% of the world population. The weight of words . . . I am alone with my (s)word, loaded with the black on white of verbs and nouns and I write, as others are writing, to try to put words to an act entirely stripped of sense and yet full of meaning.

Special bulletin, Montreal, Wednesday December sixth, 1989, 18:00 hours. "A mad gunman has opened fire on students at the Polytechnique in an unexplainable act." The terse communiqué falls on this glacial evening in Quebec like a cold shower: the clean and neat environment of the Polytechnique has been completely turned upside down, the future geniuses of industry have been threatened, someone has shot at the future of Quebec. Worse, somebody has committed murder, right here at home, and not just in *Allô Police*. It does no good to switch from one station to another, looking for someone to say it isn't so. For once, all the stations are in agreement: violence is at the door, violence exists right here, twelve kilometers or two steps away from home.

And then, the shock—the more time goes on, the more the students on the screen transform themselves into women students, regardless of Grevisse and the other French grammarians who would block a generalized feminization of the language. And the more the students become *women* students, the more the implacable truth breaks through. It isn't future engineers who are shot down, it is women, because the killer sees them as feminists. Logic wavers, the image on the TV screen blurs, and this is not so much a threat for the future than an entire history of violence and terror threatening to resurface in the present, to show us that we must start all over again and that there will always be one to whom it wasn't properly explained.

But explain what? What is there to understand? How to draw up a beautifully structured analysis when they're firing on you at point-blank range? In the confusion, one utters something useless, what should be said is forgotten, and subtleties are dropped. We rely on the living breathing body to articulate its reaction and, when all is said and done, there really are so few words in the language.

We are vulnerable and that virus, the media, always takes advantage of catastrophes to insinuate itself into people's opinions. Those who are holding the big end of the microphone don't miss their chance to speak their mind, and they go on to share with us some truly personal opinions about life, love, and death. I remember trying, like many others, to persuade myself that this was a chance happening brought about by a sick individual. But I could not force myself to believe this.

I see myself struggling against the terrible truth which tried to slip itself into each line of the communiqué I was writing. I was struggling along with other women who, like myself, were driven by an indelible sense of rage mixed with powerlessness, to attempt to organize the events on paper so that they would make sense. I think of other women like us in every part of Quebec, and all over the world, forming the same letters, the same words, caught up in the same contradictory thoughts. We imagined the worst, yet we clung desperately to the most blind hope, and we wrote it, as one unanimous "I":

> Fourteen women were executed at the Polytechnique, several others wounded. Their crime: that they were women? That they were students in a discipline traditionally reserved for men? I think (I WANT TO BELIEVE IT, I want desperately to believe) that it was an isolated act, that the killer belongs to no particular group, that his act represents no general way of thinking. But one thing we know for sure: a man has killed some women. It appears that he set up the following equation: woman student in Engineering = non-traditional vocation = potential feminist = danger. I wept in front of my television set, from horror and from compassion. Then, as an activist, I sobbed with rage. How far do we have to go to make them understand?[1]

But men, the worthy representatives of the patriarchy, feared that we might become horribly frightened. It was absolutely essential that all steps be taken to immediately dismantle any fragment of hypothesis before it could begin to be articulated. I can still hear them, wildly conjecturing, dissecting the psychological entrails of the murderer. To be sure, they had to put words, their words, around the event as soon as possible. They had to over-semanticize it, even if they were wrong, just to take up the entire semantic space—we will leave not a single centimetre free, lest a dissenting interpretation take hold.

It was in this manner that, using their patriarchal tools of analysis, the killer rapidly became an unhappy young man who was the victim of a miserable childhood and it was all his mother's fault. Paradoxically, attempts were made to make women feel guilty for not having thought about the poor mother of the murderer. There was even a journalist who wanted to blame everything on our consumer society's worship of beauty which, he claimed, would have dealt to the killer an unhappy, loveless existence. The mind reels as it watches the patriarchal system clutch at every semblance of a clue. The killer is not only a misogynist, he is stark raving mad, and there must have been a woman in there somewhere who contributed to his disturbance. This is how the media, the patriarchy's instrument, manages to make victims of torturers.

The words of news bulletins—those choice implacable bullets—pierce public opinion. The event was quickly reduced to a family quarrel which blew out of proportion, and the public act took on personal dimensions. Then, all of a sudden, this violence became something new which is exercised against women who, "wrongly," experienced a deep sense of injustice. And the denials, silencers used to hush up the main points, had to be seen to be believed. Each man, each woman spoke from his or her own sense of guilt, his or her own sense of victim, when the evidence was right there, enough to break your heart, enough to shock your eyes out of their sockets.

Sure, the killer had serious psychological problems. Certainly a "normal" man will not go so far as to kill women just because he's angry with them. Sure, we had a madman in our midst. However, we must examine the significance of the targets—after all, this individual projected his hate fantasies against them!

The more we think about it—the more I think about it—the more there's a connection to be made between this extreme manifestation and the aura of animosity which tarnishes the everyday confrontations of men and women, however we wish to name them. And let's admit it, the reactions of certain men confirm our feelings. They demonstrate their aggression in an attempt to prove to us, at all cost, that we are wrong.

In fact, when it became obvious that not one article, not one news column, not one public affairs program and not one editorial would succeed in convincing all of us in one fell swoop that we should not interpret this as a deliberate blow to women, rather than to students who happened to be women, the engines suddenly went into reverse, and some men began to endorse our interpretation of the facts in order to justify what the killer had done. It was true, the murderer had killed women because he saw them as feminists, but wasn't this because feminism had been vindictive, wasn't it because we feminists had gone too far? They even managed to round up a few lost individuals who confessed to their approval of his revolting deed (except that, in their opinion, it was a tactical error to make such a blatant gesture.)

To crown it all, a rumour began to spread that the feminist movement had seen in this event an opportunity to further its cause. Not only were we wrong to "take it personally," to feel that our integrity as women had been attacked, but we were manipulating a tragic incident for political purposes. Men even accused us of attacking their sensitivity by expressing ourselves publicly, and justified their aggressive counter-reactions by pointing to accusations which, they felt, had been directed toward them. And *we* were taking it "personally"? No more please, I'm choking on it!

However, even if our feelings were those of rage, which we had no intention of silencing and channelled into our writing, the fact remains that fourteen women were murdered by a man. Good grief! We said it! We said it out loud!

Two months later the feeling hadn't changed; it simply made itself known in all senses and across all registers. I spoke of contradictory thoughts, collective grief, deep pain, but linear language doesn't always know how to render opinions that require conjugating, feelings that are multi-layered, reactions that dovetail and cross over into each other. Sixty days later, what happened fell into place as whole knowledge. Tragically, it took on meaning and, in doing so, it echoed a social structure that is examined and rectified far less often than is generally believed.

This massacre has etched itself into the continuum of daily violence against women, which the media doesn't always tell us about. There's not enough space (there are always so many political spats and hockey games). All men are not killers, and killers don't kill only women, but women are always killed by men. One woman a week is beaten to death by the man who promised her the sky, just like the men in the Harlequin Romances she read between fights with him. My friend is raped in the street between the corner store and home. But walls are thick and windows airtight. Our TV set brings the world into our home at suppertime, but no TV news program makes much of these little acts of violence. Murder is always harder to take when it's one of our own. How many women's lives have been deleted across the ages, symbolically or in actual fact, without anything being done about it, because the tools of history and society lay in the hands of the patriarchy?

A lot of women weren't killed that day. They were killed before and they are killed every day: our colleagues harassed by a man, our sisters beaten by a man, our neighbours murdered by a man, our friends raped by a man, our mothers kept ignorant by men. In newspapers and on television everything possible is done to make sure that women do not recognize, in each incident of violence, the symptom of a much more significant malaise. To think that when a woman is murdered by her spouse the act is called "a crime of passion!" This is how the reality of brute violence is diverted from public consciousness. We are educated about men's violence toward women with a cumulative clever blend of repression-expression.

> Having a woman's body today often means being the object of violence—direct and personal domestic violence and the pernicious act which is rape; and widespread and impersonal violence in certain forms of pornography and screen images on television and in cinema.[2]

Violence against women is projected even in the news of the world transmitted by our media. Now if I say that the media is an instrument of the patriarchy, this is because it relies on image and language systems established in favour of the patriarchy. How could the media not transmit a false or, at best, limited image of our reality when our existence is not taken into account by the media's lexical and even grammatical options? All this misogyny, whether on a small or large scale, is an open door to violence. To go from a sexist language to the subordination of women in a given society requires only a few small steps.

In refusing to classify the women students as women, and by referring to them just as students, a sub-class was created. This was the first manifestation in a long process aimed at withholding from this event the status of violence committed by a man against women. This is a pure and simple gesture that nullifies the identity of women, and is then written into the aftermath of the initial act. Women have the right to be subjects in their own right, certainly, but only with copula verbs, as in the antidiluvian "Be beautiful and keep quiet." They have a certain access to non-traditional roles but only if they accept being called a lady busdriver, a woman judge, a woman Governor-General, and so on—just as the newspapers call them. Here we have an instance where, even in the singular, the masculine takes precedence over the feminine, for the function supercedes the individual. This is how, with or without force, women are denied the position of subjects in their own right.

Even as I write this text, I come up against the sexism of the language. For instance, the moment I try to turn the Polytechnique murder situation around, I find my vocabulary limited by the patriarchy: "misogynist" does not exist in a feminine version. We hate women but, as if it has no meaning, we do not—with a way of thinking encapsulated in one word—hate men. If we do have such hatred, we demonstrate aversion toward "Men," toward human beings, and we are "misanthropists." A misogynist hates women's difference, while a woman has no right to feel contempt for what, in her view, embodies this difference, since according to the dictionary she would be hating her own gender. A great many women have never recovered from this particular double bind.

I would also like to point out that we would be wrong to underestimate the part language plays in the feminist struggle. Words are not everything, but they are far from being unimportant, and if they show themselves to be deceptive, well, that axe cuts both ways. What was missing from the aftermath of December 6 were the right words, spoken as quickly as possible. What we had were agents of the patriarchy, with their paraphernalia already in place, made to measure and channelled into the media, conceived by them and for them. I am not saying that women remained silent, I am not saying that feminists were not allowed to express themselves publicly, I am simply lamenting the fact that there was so little space made for a feminist perspective in the forums allocated to listeners and viewers, and that in the sacred name of objective journalism, any point of view that was not based on common (patriarchal) sense was at a marked disadvantage.

Usage is what affects the transformation of a language, and in speaking we find a way to make sense of the world. It all comes down to usage. Each time we try to make a word nonsexist, we struggle with the social fabric which revels in it. Each word we articulate is a step toward making language work for us, a step toward a means of communicating. It is extremely important to speak up at all public forums, even if we are accused of rattling on, complaining, saying the same thing over and over again, taking advantage of certain situations to promote feminism, etc. There's so much violence yet to be exposed.

Thus, in spite of it all, I take action by speaking, for my "consoeurs" and for some of my confreres—even if everyone doesn't take all of it into consideration. I write to name the acts and deeds of my world, in order that we stop calling a doe a deer, a mare a horse. I write to try to eke out my place in history, to contribute to the making of a different history, a good one this time, to scream out the centuries of hidden violence. Words—so useless and yet so full of meaning, so full of repercussions. I write to endow us with a subjectivity that will be none other than our very selves. I, alone, in the name of ten, a hundred, a thousand women—but also for myself—I write. To prevent my world from making my existence (completely) null and void.

Notes

1. From a special edition of the student newspaper at the University of Quebec at Montreal, December 7, 1989

2. CLIO Collective, *Four Centuries of the History of Women in Quebec*, Montreal, Quinze, 1892, p. 496

A Little Story of Censorship

Ginette Bastien and Renée Ouimet

Thursday, December 7, 1989

Dear Ginette,
I won't be able to write you today. This murder of fourteen women has totally devastated me. Write back anyway; maybe you will have found the right words. Renée.

Friday, December 8, 1989

Renée,
I understand why you feel helpless. Alas, words fail me too. I was working at the University of Montreal the night before last. All those women murdered and the women students, the women who work there, the female teachers, all of them, absolutely devastated. The confusion, the indignation, the anger. "It's all right. Everything's under control," they told us at work. What do you mean, control? Whose control? What's being controlled? I'll write again soon. Ginette.

Friday afternoon

Ginette,
I'd love to just stay home and be still, but I have to get myself to a union meeting to prepare the next issue of the Association's newsletter. My mind is swimming with the recent events and I'm full of anger: we cannot tolerate violence anymore, even the most subtle kind. That's why I've decided to write a short article for the union membership. In it, I'm writing things that you know already—things that I think are important to emphasize. Such as saying that what the killer did is not an "isolated gesture," it's only more "spectacular" and more sensational than rape, incest, and other day-to-day violence. I'm also writing because only when we've individually and collectively spoken out against the remarks and acts that are violent toward women, and against the pornography and violence in the media, will we really feel free of all responsibility for such acts. Of course, the executive's editorial commitee approves of my initiative as well as the content of my article. I'll keep you posted. Renée.

Sunday, December 10

Hi Renée,

I agree with you: we have to protest. Every article, every letter, every phone call counts. I spoke up at Métropolis this afternoon, at the gathering against the federal abortion law proposal. It seemed to me necessary to make the connection with the Polytechnique, since "forced maternity" is precisely a form of subtle violence sanctioned by repressive male laws. It's too bad you couldn't have been there this afternoon. It was comforting—the crowd silent and attentive, moved by what I said. Some insightful comments were made. There were some men there; a few of them were right on. I'll give you the details when I see you. G.

Monday, December 11

Ginette,

You won't believe what happened. It's unbelievable. I have to tell somebody about this; if not, I'm going to choke on it. Listen to this!

A colleague from the editorial committee changed her mind about my article; she heard a "a feminist" on TV say we ought to keep our mouths shut, or else we might provoke more violence! I was surprised, but not really. I knew, in any case, that my text was going to be rejected and that this would be our paper's first case of censorship. I insisted that the other members of the executive vote by phone. It was critical. The outcome? I have only two allies left. The reactions of the others were even more disgusting than I could have imagined. Remember the guy I told you about? He told me I shouldn't say "fourteen women were killed . . . " Honest! That's what he said. "You must say fourteen *people*," that's what he said to me. "Your article is going to incite violence, it's going to make some of our members get violent. On the other hand, it's a good idea to offer our condolences to the families; that part, you can leave in." A second colleague said exactly the same thing to me, but in a different way. Another one told me to make more *positive* remarks. For example, to say that this man, the killer, was possibly sick. And so on and so forth.

I refuse to be quiet. I am not going to shelve this article. What to do. Quit? Publicly accuse the union executive, of which I am the president? Publish the article somewhere else? I just lost, in one fell swoop, all interest in working with men and women who deny women's reality. All of this just proves that what that killer did was not an isolated act. Tonight I'm sad, but it does me good to write. I know that I'm not alone. Renée.

Wednesday, December 13

Hi there, Ginette!

Here I am again with the next episode of my adventure! I just discussed what happened with my article with the Status of Women Committee of the union's head office. They found it staggering. They thought, like a lot of people, that those who practice alternative medicine were "a separate breed," "OK" people, "cool," "sensitized," you know? It's always the same story . . . the ones at the Head Office always tell me I have to "educate" the others. I've had it! I don't feel like educating! Teach the guys in the union as well as carry on the political work? Sounds a lot like having a job at work and a job at home. Not me, no way!

Found a solution for my article: It'll be published in the Head Office bulletin, signed Renée Ouimet, President of . . . What did my executive say? I found out at the meeting when I told them about my having approached the Head Office. Nobody seemed particularly disturbed—the article could be published anywhere except in "our newspaper". Then, politely, in a totally awkward social blur, we proceeded to the first order of business. I went home, disappointed. They'd understood absolutely nothing. Bye, Renée.

Wednesday, December 13

Dear Renée,

It was predictable that condemning violence would let loose all kinds of little violent incidents in our lives, even our private lives. That's the history of the feminist struggle!

As for your cool, sensitized colleagues there—I despise their kind. They're candy-coated. Scratch the surface and underneath is a real pill. When it suits them, they go along with feminist proposals. When it doesn't, they rip them to pieces. Whatever you do, don't discuss it. RIP THEM TO PIECES. Bye, G.

Thursday, December 14

Ginette,

A new turn of events. Phone call early this morning from the guy I told you about: " Renée, I couldn't sleep all night. I kept feeling like I'd been made a fool of, and I had some pretty violent feelings toward you, like Lépine. You can just go to hell, goddamn it!" Those are exactly the words he used. I was speechless. My action had had some impact after all: a member of the executive was threatening me for having denounced violence and all those who are too afraid to speak out against it. Terrorist politics. A blurred threat that smelled of death. I'm not surprised. That's life, our life, it would appear. Write me before you leave, I need it. Renée.

Thursday, December 14

Renée,

Don't let their secretive, masked terrorism get even a toehold. It's typical of them—rough somebody up in their personal life. That's so much easier . . .

And Christmas is coming . . . Are we going to go through with it, yet again? I hope that these few months away will bring me peace. Keep writing to me, even if I'm not there. I'll read your letters all at once when I get back. Be brave. Ginette.

Wednesday, January 24, 1990

Ginette,

When I got back after the Holidays, I told the executive about the December 14 phone call. I refuse to let this drop. Nobody reacted. The guy I told you about spoke up and repeated in front of the others the terrible things he said to me over the phone. SILENCE. Nobody reacted. Not one man, not one woman. The aggressor had their support. Clearly, the members of the executive prefer to keep silent, rather than break the illusion of "harmonious" relations. For quite a few minutes, I didn't know what to do anymore. Everyone had let me down. Because of their fear of confrontation, their laziness, their cowardice, because of human stupidity. Let down, period. I went back home, and I couldn't sleep. I was publicly accosted, and nobody reacted . . . Renée.

February, 1990

Ginette,

No new drama since the last one, but the same little tale keeps making its rounds day after day. I no longer know what stance I should take. They want me to feel guilty. For what? For refusing to accept violence. You were so right when you told me that if we keep quiet, we encourage violence, and if we speak up, we could very easily find ourselves violently confronted! "Privately," my two allies said they now consider they *should have* reacted . . .

I continue to keep up a polite rapport with them, given the importance of the union, but I am not at all convinced that this is the right solution! You know, I am soon going to publish a text that will tell the story of what happened to me. Do you think I was right to keep their names out of it? Say, when are you coming back? Renée.

THIS IS NOT THE FIRST TIME

This letter appeared in La Presse on December 10, 1989.

Feminists All!

Micheline Dumont

They died protesting that they were not feminists. He singled them out, took aim and killed them, because they were all feminists.

What tragic hatred! Faced with such demented violence, are we supposed to be content with expressing our helplessness? No, perhaps we should go beyond sharing the pain of so many unjustly wounded families. Should we therefore demand more laws, more control? Should we go into mourning with all flags at half-mast?

First, we must have the courage to name what has happened. Feminism has become an option one cannot admit to. The young twenty-year-olds think feminism is no longer necessary. They think it was good for their mothers, who had to fight for their rights. And so it was.

We must however ask ourselves why the epithet "feminist" has become an insult. It has become an insult because men have made it one and because women have given in, once again, to this subtle and enterprising domination.

Since the beginning of time, women have been caught in a programmed concept of "woman," and have been despised collectively as "women."

A mere two decades ago women undertook a political analysis of their subordination. Men immediately felt singled out as individuals. Their retort was prompt: "Feminists! All of them!" And so it was that this rallying call began to be used against those who initially proclaimed it. It was also used against those who asserted their independence, those who condemned violence, those who entered men's territory, those who believed we'd achieved equality, those who naïvely believed that love wasn't usually an act of domination.

Feminists all! We must never forget that it was this cry that gave direction to the murderous rage of the Polytechnique killer. We must never forget that these victims committed the unforgiveable crime of choosing a male profession and a faculty where men are the majority—a faculty that, according to all the studies, women have difficulty entering. How many women are there at the Polytechnique? Five hundred? Six hundred? Seven hundred? It doesn't matter. We know now that there are fourteen less.

December 6, 1989 Among the Centuries

Nicole Brossard

I wouldn't go so far as to say they are all clowns
some accommodate the rest as they tumble in despair
Louky Bersianik

On this sixth of December in 1989, I am slowly drifting through blue luminous Paris, rue des Archives between the grey stones, rue des Blancs-Manteaux, and I am not thinking of what it's like in Montreal. I am on Paris time, no jet lag, and headed for a rendez-vous with a Lebanese woman who is a student. She will be talking to me about a horror that is inconceivable to anyone who comes from such a peaceful place it is not yet called a country. Yes, I come from a place where the blood and clabbering noises made by humans in the pain of mass death haven't yet entered the site where words are formed.

That day I was walking slowly, following my usual habit of looking only at women as if to reassure myself about humanity. I walk in the full light of day. I have no reason to think of death. I have no intention of thinking of death. Paris is blue. Montreal is far away and covered with snow. I walk in absolute reality.

On December 7, 1989, I learn that a man has just killed fourteen women. The man, they say, separated the men and the women into two groups. The man called the women feminists; he voiced his hatred toward them. The man fired. The women dropped. The other men ran away. Suddenly,

I/they are dead
felled by a
break in meaning.

A WOMAN WHO IS CRYING OUT IN PAIN CAN SHE HEAR AT THE SAME TIME THE CRY OF ANOTHER WOMAN? THE CRY OF A WOMAN AND OF ANOTHER AND THE CRY OF ANOTHER WOMAN DO THEY COME TOGETHER COLLIDE IN SPACE AND TIME, THE DEEP CRY OF THE REBEL AND THE WAILING CRIES OF THE DOCILE DO THEY COME TOGETHER COLLIDE SO THAT IT WOULD SEEM ONE HEARS ONLY ONE IMMENSE LONG HORRIBLE SOUND?

DOUBT IN PARENTHESIS

The discourse, the analyses, and the commentaries that followed the massacre at the Polytechnique remind us that misogyny, phallocentrism, and ordinary sexism form such a cohesive politico-cultural whole that it is difficult to identify each man's actual participation in the oppression of women. The reasonable doubt each man benefits from has, as a consequence, the invalidation of every generalization that can be made about men's behaviour toward women, and thus it reinforces the presumed innocence of them all. In any case, given this "innocence," any well-intentioned liberal man can not only support feminist claims based on principles of equality and social justice but, all the while, discredit feminist research, analysis, and thought. Disturbing research which has discovered mass graves marking out the history of women; analysis which invalidates the foundations of patriarchal laws; creative thinking which, in the maze of paradoxes, contradictions, and hate metaphors of both fear and attraction employed by men to *domesticate the creature*, strives to understand the reasons why and the magnitude of men's hatred toward women—these work away at the very principle of life.

THE CONSISTENT HOSTILITY OF THE *INNOCENTS*

Misogyny, phallocentrism, sexism and anti-feminism are four words which could seem to be easily interchangeable. It would be, however, a serious mistake to confuse one for another, for they play very specific but oh so complementary roles when it comes to the alienation, domination, and exploitation of women.

Misogyny

Misogyny, which is hatred or contempt for women, is so pervasive throughout both history and everyday life that even women hesitate to attest to the extent of it. It is so taken for granted that most of them see in it only traditions, mores, customs, harmless proverbs, good jokes; it is so commonly accepted that philosophers, novelists, and poets have been able to write the worst inanities about women without anyone asking them to justify what they wrote, the way no one asked Céline, Heidegger and others to justify themselves with regard to anti-semitism. All men are not active misogynists but they all carry the virus. The misogynist virus is particularly prone to activate itself when a man encounters one or more women who are recalcitrant, particularly with regard to sexism. Misogyny constitutes a semantic corpus to which every man experiencing a love crisis, or a lack of argument to justify his privileges, sooner or later reverts. Misogyny allows women to be at once humiliated and dubbed inferior. Active misogyny nourishes the corpus, passive misogyny resorts to it, depending on the circumstances.

Phallocentrism

Opposite misogyny, which degrades women and dubs them inferior, phallocentrism enhances men's worth and deifies them, on the basis of the phallus fantasized as supreme signifier. *Me ego phallus we are Man.* Cultivated over thousands of years, phallocentrism provides justification for God, his emissaries, and all his representatives to be male. Phallocentrism explains why social organization is conceived and arranged according to the needs, fantasies, comfort, and sexuality of men (even those who are at the bottom of the scale). Phallocentrism reinforces in each man the certitude that each piece of power he holds by virtue of his maleness is *naturally* justified. Phallocentrism is a corpus to which all men avail themselves when the time comes to talk ontology, epistemology, ethics, and morality.

Sexism

Sexism, which is a discriminatory attitude and practice with regard to women, is so well integrated into our mores that we are able to refer to it as "ordinary." Indeed, sexism is always ordinary for it normalizes, makes the imaginary constructs "misogyny" and "phallocentrism" commonplace in our everyday life. Sexism is an instruction manual to which men refer in order to manage the unavoidable reality of the difference between the sexes, with regard to sexuality, reproduction, and work. Sexism is "male politics,"* male management of personal and public life. Alongside the misogynist who consciously thinks and propagates his hatred for women and the phallocrat who fantasizes the superiority of the male, is the sexist, who profits from, protects, and perpetuates the privileges, honours, and advantages which for him are the equivalent of the pathological hatred and delusions of grandeur that respectively characterize the other two. Sexists are ordinary

---

* *The expression is borrowed from the French translation of Kate Millet's* **Sexual Politics,** *translated as* **La Politique du mâle**

men that women recognize one at a time without ever being able to get an idea of their actual numbers.

Anti-feminism

Anti-feminism is the *political response* of men to the *political voice* of women, which has finally come into its own in the public sphere. Contrary to the ordinary sexism practiced generally by men in a relaxed manner, anti-feminism is a defensive reaction, which obliges men to make a fuss publicly and to flex the miso-phallo-sexist muscle which backs up their argument. It is rather interesting to note that, following the massacre at the Polytechnique, it took only a few feminists voicing their opinion for the majority of male commentators to manifest their hostile anti-feminism.

In summary, the events at the Polytechnique are there to remind us that from *male politics* (misogyny, phallocentrism, and ordinary sexism) to *men's political response* (anti-feminism), this is self-evident: men are just as hostile to women when they make no demands (women) as when they claim their rights (feminists), whether women pay attention to them (heterosexuals), or ignore them (lesbians).

YOUNG WOMEN AND VERTIGO

This permanent hostility men have toward women, this is what we forget about when the sky is blue, that is what those survivors—who were so quick to declare they weren't feminists—had forgotten. What, in fact, did they actually mean to say? Did they want to disassociate themselves from women who fight against unjust laws, against violence against women, against the degradation of women's image? Did they want to make it clear they were not lesbians, that they were not against men? Did they think, as the media would have us believe, that feminists are a category of undesirable women whose perspective is narrow and partisan, whose words are bitter and excessive, and whose bad will does enormous harm to the "women's rights" the majority of women would be interested in? Did they think that feminists threaten the "harmonious" relations between men and women? But what can a woman be thinking of when she says, "I'm not a feminist"? What hasn't she thought of? Who hasn't she thought of?

SEXIST QUEBEC TRAGEDY?

The question is delicate, and nothing is less certain than our ability to answer it properly. Yet a large part of our incredulity, our stupor before the fact, and our shame at the Polytechnique massacre can be related to this question: how could such a thing happen in Quebec? Are Quebec men more sexist than the rest, do they feel more threatened, ripped off, or rejected by feminism? Has Quebec feminism known such success that we must now speak of a "suppressed" sexist misogyny? To these questions, I cannot respond. I can only note that in no other population with Roman Catholic traditions has feminism so rapidly influenced people's private lives and the social and cultural reality, in no other *French language* population has feminism been able to fight publicly, and with a certain success, sexism in language and advertising. But, it will be said no doubt, men here are able to listen to what feminists say. Yes, it is true there is a certain audience, but what is more important is that Quebec society has had to acquire in thirty years all the important currents of thought founded on principles of liberation (the ideology of decolonization, secularization, the counter-culture, Marxism, feminism), all the while educating itself in order to be transformed and to conquer its identity. In other words, Quebec feminism was able to develop and take its place in the public sphere more easily because it was part of an immense liberation movement, because it happened at the strategic moment of Quebec's arrival on the world scene as a modern *North American* society.

BRIEF EVIDENCE

The stream of remarks, attitudes, and reactions that followed the massacre remind us that:

only feminist claims which are based on principles of equality and social justice can, in the end, be heard by liberal society

despite certain social gains and the liberalism of some men, the solidarity of feminists, that is, of lesbians and women, still remains our only hope of changing reality

women's lack of solidarity with feminists and lesbians attests to a symbolic split whose principal consequence is to reinforce the patriarchal clan in its ideology and its privileges

feminists have nothing to gain by softening their intentions in order to give themselves a good media image the feminist movement must be visibly present all the time and not just during moments of crisis, such as the massacre at the Polytechnique and the Daigle-Tremblay affair*

anti-feminists should be identified as political enemies

whatever the complexity of human reality and motivations, nothing can excuse or justify sexist violence and discrimination. Furthermore, any biological or psychological explanation which aims to excuse men's violent behaviour toward women would be much more serious, for it would lead us to believe that men are incurable criminals.

*   *see note page 68*

On this 6th of February, 1990, Montreal is grey. I have a rendez-vous with a student. She will be young. I know that she will talk to me about literature, a little about herself, about life. I know that we can't say everything at once. I know that she has no reason to be thinking about death. Yet I know that she knows that if it were not for the deep cry of the rebel and the long wail of the docile, no one would care about the hard and violent sounds that haunt our collective memory.

I walk along in Montreal. Every step I take pushes back the shadow.

Killing as Divine Sacrifice

Andrée Matteau

*An insane system is not one which has no ethics, it is a
system which cannot escape the immorality of its ethics.*

From the seventh to the twenty-third of December, 1989, six
out of the twelve women who entered my consulting room for their
weekly appointment spontaneously spoke of their feelings
regarding the traumatic events of December six.

"What happened at the Polytechnique, that really got me down.
Before, *I* was the one who had violence to contend with—not *all*
women. Once I got clear of my own personal violence, nobody was
supposed to be able to touch me, right? But what happened at the
Polytechnique really upset me. Right from the very first night, I had
my own interpretation of what the media was saying. There was no
place for women in the media. My daughter was trembling, she was
nauseated. I said to myself: what's going to happen to our girls?
The battle of the sexes carried out with guns? I feel helpless. I
thought I was making a new life for myself, one without violence.
It's not true." (L., 40 years old)

"The Polytechnique tragedy, now that's horrifying. It's the
fin-de-siècle decadence, the end of a civilization. I couldn't even
read the papers or watch the TV." (S., 44 years old)

"The Wednesday of the murders, I wept. The killer's reasoning?
That women had taken his place. A lot of men feel threatened. At the
office, men don't want a woman boss." (L., 37 years old)

"The tragedy at the Polytechnique, now that really threw me.
Yesterday on the phone to my boyfriend I said that men haven't
changed. Women are still beaten, raped, 'incestuated,' killed. It's
demoralizing for the children. Men haven't come nearly as far as
they would like us to think. They hate women." (S., 26 years old)

In contrast, I heard not a single comment from the eleven men I
saw in consultation during the same period. Was this a rule of
silence? An ostrich syndrome? Indifference? Emotion-proof virility?
Numbness with regard to women's social condition? Guilt?

I thought of all those other women who, like my clients, felt
they'd been dealt a blow to their spirit and their guts, the women
who identified with "slain human being." I thought of my
colleagues, my women friends, my daughter, my daughter's

friends. Yes, I thought of my daughter. Crying, she asked me to observe the minute of silence.

I thought of my anger at belonging to this civilization which, since the beginning of time, has violated part of humanity to satisfy its thirst for conquest, power, control, victory, possession, aggression, virility, all in the name of law, religion, sexuality, science, politics, economics, madness.

"He's insane," we declared. "This is only an isolated incident," we proclaimed. The "we" in question pleaded *insanity* in order to mask the symbolic significance of these crimes.

And once again I called my practice into question! For twelve years, I have listened to women tell me how they are obliterated by patriarchal authority, sometimes in the spirit of sacrifice, often as a form of obedience, but mostly they acquiesce in order to survive. The fear, the insecurity, is pervasive.

Women's sexuality is obliterated on the altar of patriarchy.

The institutionalization of heterosexual coitus—translated into law 2,500 years ago in order to increase the population and consolidate through the use of arms the holdings on the desired property—continues to this day to define sexuality. Sexual pleasure is defined according to male criteria. Forced to be passive, women are rendered inferior; different from men, women are made to feel guilty. Female sexuality is denied, and male sexuality benefits.

"I am frigid. I am not normal. I am afraid my partner will abandon me if I don't respond to his sexual needs three or four times a week." In this unequal relationship, the woman is afraid. From this point of view, the sexual act embodies one of the most oppressive and exploitative acts in our society. It represents the age-old symbol of male appropriation of women. "My wife doesn't enjoy sex. I brought her here to get cured."

The institution of male orgasm by penetration permits men to believe they are the owners of women's children and of women's bodies. If a woman does not submit to coitus, a man will exert his right by force, domination, aggression, control, and violence.

The liberty of women and children is obliterated on the altar of patriarchy.

The institutionalization of conjugal violence, incest, rape and sexual assault is programmed into the patriarchal system, a system which is generally accepting of violence in a heterosexual relationship. "My husband beats me. My religious beliefs do not allow me to ask for a divorce."

It is a system in which the male domination of women is masked by the paradigm of the family (take incest, for example), and permitted, even admired, in the context of social, financial, and sexual relations. Incest, rape and sexual assault are but an extension of the violence in interpersonal relations, relationships in which women are programmed for submission and obedience—programmed to remain the property of men. In this way, the aggressor is only repeating the customary social scenario, and to encourage him in this "we" provide him with the necessary cerebral supplies, which go by the name of "fantasies" and are distributed largely by the media, as advertising, film, literature, etc.

The humanity of women is obliterated on the altar of patriarchy.

The institutionalization of pornography in fact presupposes the superiority of men, through the glorification of the coital act. It also presupposes the physical possession of women, and that the use of women's bodies for reproduction is a natural right for men. In the end, the ideology of pornography reveals that it is men's sexual will which defines the parameters of women's sexual being, just as it defines their entire identity. "It doesn't bother me that my husband watches porno films; he finds them entertaining, and they do him good."

Pornography is central to the male sexual system. It is part of those institutions which control the sexual and reproductive use of women's bodies, just as the law does—in partnership with marriage, prostitution, health, economy, organized religion, and systematic physical violence against women.

Life is obliterated under patriarchal authority. The institutionalization of power over life represents the patriarchal system's ethics. In this binary ethics, women are associated with nature and men with culture—a culture which then imposes its power over nature by attempting to control it.

Weapons have historically been the preferred means of exercising control and representing culture. As a Vietnam veteran once stated during a TV program[1]: "This is my rifle; this is my gun. One is for killing, the other for fun!" The killer at the Polytechnique used a weapon instead of his penis! This act was motivated by both the sexual and cultural aggression of the killer himself and by the power our culture exerts over women. His goal was to obliterate the disobedience, the deviance, of women. And in a final magnanimous gesture, out of reverence for power, the killer sacrificed himself to this divinity.

In such a sociopolitical context, as in certain therapeutic situations, to suggest that a client take one step more could lead to suicide. Obstacles of a sexual, emotional, social, intellectual and spiritual nature are still too great. It is in this way that I recognize limits to what therapy can do.

In exceptional circumstances, some women can negotiate their survival (if nothing more) by learning to sacrifice their identity, to obey and to step out of harm's way. This is what those fourteen women had learned how to do, against their own will, perhaps. They deserved, therefore, to be but back in their place on the mantle of patriarchy. They were not deserters!

During the funeral, I too observed the minute of silence, all the while reformulating in my own mind the words I was hearing: "They were born of the Mother; they were penetrated, dismembered, dessicated, rendered null and void by the Father . . . just as in a snuff film."[2]

Notes

1. The January 9, 1990 broadcast of *Parler pour Parler*, presented on Radio-Québec, was dedicated to Vietnam veterans.

2. Pornographic films, circulating illegally in the United States, in which the protagonists, always women, are murdered, usually having been dismembered or gutted. The enormous success of these films—apparently filmed in South America—was due to the fact (confirmed by the media) that the deaths were real. This has never been officially proven, but the fact that people believed they were real and revelled in this knowledge was sufficient to incite the anger of American feminists. (Editors' note)

REFERENCES

Bersianik, Louky. "L'éprouvette porteuse" in *Sortir de la maternité du laboratoire*. Status of Women Council, Quebec government, Quebec, 1988, p. 385-387

Dworkin, Andrea. *Pornography, Men Possessing Women*. Perigee Books, New York, 1981

French, Marilyn. *Beyond Power*. Ballantine, New York, 1986

Ledray, Linda E. *Recovering from Rape*. Henry Holt & Co., New York, 1986.

Matteau, Andrée. "Ode aux pornocrates" in *Les cahiers du socialisme*, No. 16. Montreal, 1985, p. 6-9

Contempt Will Have Had its Day

Marie Savard

the beauty in the sleeping woods
is made of a piece of plank
made of a piece of shank
but crowned with angel's hair

courtesans of this land
themselves courted
somewhere around here
the night before being killed
descend upon us today
at high noon
I think of Nathalie
of Julie
the lady in turn takes a step up
in this land
my daughter is in her grave
somewhere around here

This Wednesday in December my feelings run rampant as I hear the news of the Polytechnique killings. We learn that it was fourteen women students, the age of my daughter, who were killed by a so-called "mad gunman" whose target was feminists, women who only wanted to be themselves, as one of the victims humbly tried to tell him before he started firing. "Bunch of feminists!" he supposedly yelled, in the heat of the action. A clear message, it seems to me, which found itself echoed in the open line radio talk shows in the days following.

Next, on TV, came the swarm of psychologists and experts, momentary purveyors of the dominant thinking, attempting to explain the tragedy by the fact that the killer had problems relating to the fair sex (as if he were the only one). They cited his disturbed childhood, and (still the great herd) they concluded with thinly veiled warnings to feminists to keep still—above all warning them not to try to take advantage of this tragedy by associating it with an extremist political gesture arising from a patriarchal culture of imperative sexism. These were warnings with which both men and women interviewers managed to achieve an astonishing but nonetheless predictable consensus. There was now a forbidden analysis, a way of reading the predetermined deaths, which must not be allowed to surface. The collective psychosis, especially, must not be allowed to surface. Nevertheless, we learn from the same media that a "female extremist" had threatened, in a communiqué addressed to city hospitals, to kill male babies in their bassinets. How vulgar. Now I wonder who might stand to gain from such demagoguery, in a society where the expression "feminist extremists" circulates at will?

And in the newspapers we were treated to the most frenetic analyses. Professor Angella Terregrossa in her "Reflection on Feminism" (*Le Devoir*, December 15, 1989) would have done better to ask herself if the enemy of woman might not be the brute ignorance of man, instead of failing to acknowledge any connotation of sexual difference and reducing the feminist issue to what she considers "the real opposition—exploiter and exploited, regardless of the gender of the individuals involved." (And why not say to Blacks, "regardless of the colour of their skin . . .?") After some comments on "the loose morals" in the TV dramas of Lise Payette, this empty reasoning leads the author to a rather peculiar and far-fetched indictment of feminists who, she persists, "wage the war [she's talking about abortion] as if *all* women do not wish to bring a pregnancy to term." This should be a war waged without regard for the gender of the individuals who bring a pregnancy to term, perhaps?

And it goes on and on. Contempt has all the time in the world. It has all the time it needs to heap the worst of the tragedy at the Polytechnique onto feminists, while we try desperately to see in the killer's act only a gesture completely devoid of context—demented and gratuitous. Yet Marc Lépine's action is anything but unfortunate innocence. There is no contradiction between his act and the relentless repression of feminist thought by a dominant stream of thought, which will stay precisely where it is for as long as it can take up the space it requires. And this space is composed of the other, another, who is not made in *his* image.

Won't women, these *others*, ever get tired of this eternal status quo? Will the lingering taste of death coming from the events of this December, this ashen Wednesday, leave us terrified, mummified in the only stereotypes they expect from us? Will we keep silent and helpless in the face of the continual sacrifice of Iphigenia? It is not tears our daughters need, it is our anger.

VIOLENCE: MADNESS GREAT AND SMALL

This letter appeared in La Presse, December 20, 1989

Hey, Mister Psychiatrist!

France Lachapelle

A man killed fourteen girls and wounded fourteen other people because he had had a run-in with feminism. I am forty-years-old. I am a feminist, like most women of my generation. Yes, I struggle for a status equal to that of men. Yes, I fight for justice! Is there anything wrong with that?

I would so much like to do my job without having to do extra just to prove that I am as good as the boys. I would like very much for promotions to be more than the result of backroom scheming, or affirmative action programs. I ask only that my work merit the respect of others in my profession. And that's feminism, is it? That's so terrible that fourteen women had to be killed for it?

A psychiatrist who was a guest on the TV program *Le Point* stated that we had to look for the causes of this crime in the killer's childhood. He may have been abandoned by his mother and this would explain why he was taking his anger out on women. Oh, I know, Doctor, this is just a theory, but . . . my God! This is the first thing that comes to your mind, is it? Pray tell, from the wealth of your experience or your knowledge? Well, Mr. Expert-on-the-Conscience, if the behaviour of the mother in certain circumstances is so influential for the child, why not let a woman have the right to choose when and in what conditions she will be pregnant? Why refuse her the right to abortion on demand? Why does the medical profession make this choice for her? To my knowledge, you won't be there to help her get through the day-to-day reality of her maternity.

Mr. Psychiatrist, why didn't you point out that in the past five years volunteers who staff telephone help lines have registered a significant increase in the number of callers who are manifestly violent and who take it out verbally on women? In subtracting good as well as bad power from the male, the female sex becomes *the* cause of personal and social problems. The men who are most threatened are absolutely convinced of this. This is one explanation which deserves another, wouldn't you agree, Doctor? It happens to expand nicely upon your own.

I am a feminist, yes! And I am exhausted and worn out from these constant battles. And I'm sorry, Mr. Murderer, but I am in no way responsible for any part of the act you have committed.

No Gravestone!

Franco Chiesa

This letter appeared in Le Devoir on January 10, 1990

Cursory judgements are certainly not the exclusive privilege of Western Canadian rednecks, or any other uncouth individuals for that matter.

In this part of the land, we heard a psychiatrist declare that the crazed gunman of the Polytechnique was an innocent victim of the December 6 tragedy, with the same sympathy accorded the fourteen female students the killer had lined up against the wall. You would think the killer had, at the very most, committed a "huge mistake," for which responsibility would fall (naturally!) to society for having, among other things, refused him entrance to the Armed Forces (should they have accepted him?) and for not making it possible for him to finish his college courses. Let's hope our community college drop-outs are not all tempted to pick up a rifle to solve their problems!

Contrary to what Mr. Pinero would have us believe, the media, the *Journal de Montréal* included, directed much more attention to M.L. than they normally give to murderers and for this they are to be congratulated! The *Devoir* arts critic, no less, showed such compassion that one would wish to see some of it find its way into her attitude toward the lucky "stars" she deigns to set her sights on . . . even if she hasn't quite fourteen notches in her belt!

However, even with the very best intentions, one must not give way to a simplistic leftist view of the event—in the first place, out of intellectual rigour, and second, out of respect for the men and women who will be obliged to live with this nightmare for many years to come.

If we were to give way to such a view, why shouldn't Adolf Hitler be the ultimate innocent victim of the Holocaust? His mad penchant for killing—couldn't we blame that on emotional desertion too early in life? Was he not, in fact, a betrayed and humiliated soldier? A fourth class painter, utterly demolished by a cutting Nathalie Petrowski of the time? A German deadbeat from the 20s?

I do not claim the right to judge M.L., but let us not absolve him in quite so cavalier a manner. To do so would be, if nothing else, irresponsible. Millions of people have lived through a devastated childhood. Surely we won't inaugurate a "liberation sociology" for them, something to justify all of them becoming killers.

No gravestone for M.L.!

Lépine and the Roses: Beyond Eros

Monique Panaccio

Madness is running wild. Madness has eluded social control and is attacking the very foundations of Order. This has given rise to discourse, each with its own magnifying glass, attempting to make sense of an overtly transgressive act. We watched the extraordinary attention the media gave to retracing each step in the December 6 trajectory of Marc Lépine, with the help of eyewitness accounts—with the help of a stop-watch, practically. In the days following the massacre, it was the trajectory of Marc Lépine's private life we saw displayed in the newspapers. This time, it was his teachers and others who had known him who testified. Behind these attempts to reconstruct the path of Marc Lépine is this question: what course[1] would one have had to take in order to arrive *there*? This is the point at which all discourse comes to a complete halt, whether psychiatric, feminist, psychological or other. This is the point where a limit is irreversibly, irreparably transgressed, where the Symbolic and the Imaginary[2] topple over (they were never really battened down for Marc Lépine). This is the point where love and hate merge in the site of what is unnameable.

Who was Marc Lépine attacking? In his words, feminists. Those who take these words literally could identify there a macho response to women's independence, Lépine becoming the representative of the kind of male thinking which threatens women with execution if they reject the place which keeps them socially inferior. This is not entirely wrong, but the truth is surely not so simple.

Marc Lépine fired at an image of woman, at women who, for him, were imagined—anonymous future engineers, feminists. And he killed real women who each had a name, a past, a life, a family. He walked onto a film set[3] and mistook it for reality. He killed women whom he believed possessed something of which he himself was deprived. A hit list of women he had "in his sights" was found on his person. These were women he did not know personally, but who project an image of success and determination. Let it be said in passing that the police, in publicly disclosing the names of these women without their knowledge, unknowingly (which in no way dismisses the aggressive nature of this gesture) designated these women as targets *a second time—terrorizing them*, no doubt. It is strange then, and probably not accidental (the police would have identified more easily with these individuals) that they did not disclose the names of the policewomen on the list.

A girl I know, just becoming an adolescent, was recently trying to articulate one of those philosophical questions human beings sooner or later deliberate upon. She said that the only act which could prove that something was irrefutably hers would be the destruction of that thing. I tried unsuccessfully to make her understand that, if she did this, she would only be able to prove that the object had at one time belonged to her, for she would have deprived herself of it by that very act of destruction.[4] However, what was essential for her was not the object itself, but the proof that it had once belonged to her, even if she were to lose it—its loss being what would signify the act of possession.

As for Marc Lépine, we will know nothing of the preliminary state[5] which moved him along the path where, no longer sustained by his Imaginary, he succumbed to satisfying his desire and killed women in an indifferent manner, specifying only that they be female and at the Polytechnique. He might have gone so far as to kill them *all*, something akin to possessing them all, and thereby possessing the Mother—and in so doing, assuming the place of the cruel, all-powerful Father.[6] In his attempt to make the representatives of one of the two sexes disappear, there is the intention to abolish the irreducible difference between the sexes, an act which is a form of castration.

Indeed, how can this act be relieved of its sexual and orgiastic nature? An armed man, smiling[7] with the energy that comes of knowing one holds the power of life and death, ejaculates bursts of gunfire, mortally penetrating the bodies of women who are then riddled with bullet-holes, violated. And we, the voyeurs, hang on the words of the media, attempting to "grasp" what went on, developing various theories as to what could have happened behind closed doors. From there, how not to establish a parallel with what we can only imagine and from which we are excluded—that is, the original love scene,[8] the universal and essential fantasy, if it exists?

After the tragedy, we recognized the urgent importance of naming the person who had committed such an act, as if this naming would halt the unleashing of the Imaginary[9] in its attempt to fill the void which inevitably follows horror. To name Marc Lépine was to give a name to the horror, and maybe even to feminine horror in general. In the days following the tragedy, the obscenity of the scene—cadavres with very Real heaviness—were covered up, in funerals which deployed the expedient of the sacred,[10] based on a Word attributed to God; or in the wave of sympathy which yearned to make these murders the symbol of women's difficult struggle. Both these attempts, so different in their ideological foundations, were aiming nonetheless to humanize the scene and to reaffirm the primacy of the symbolic Order.

It would be perhaps worthwhile at this point to briefly reiterate certain psychoanalytic concepts which I used earlier and which often circulate in what could be called a chaotic fashion outside their theoretical context, resulting sometimes in a confusion of languages. It would, however, be illusory to think that what follows could be regarded as a summary which would take into account all of psychoanalytic theory—for that must be associated with clinical practice.

The phallus is what comes to signify a loss. Lacan has called it the signifier of desire.[11] It is not to be confused with the penis, though the presence of the penis at times permits man to deny castration, and its absence in women is a visual prototype which can become the basis for psychic representation. In this context, castration is meant to be understood as a *representation* which has nothing to do with the actual mutilation of a body, but which is related to the feeling of inadequacy experienced by human beings of both sexes. The relationship to castration (which is the basis of the symbolic order) takes shape differently, depending on whether one is male or female. The concept of castration is a way of naming a *psychic experience*, on which is founded acknowledgement of the difference between the sexes. Castration designates the break with the mother's body, the point of no-return, and signifies the prohibition of incest, which allows the subject to enter into existence in the realm of desire, in the symbolic order, and thus in the social order by what Lacan calls the Name of the Father—i.e. by making of language a being in itself: that is, human. Ensconced in this renunciation of *jouissance* are to be found the origins of any subject, any society. The introduction of the Name of the Father comes to signify that the child, once past his *infant*[12] stage, will never again be *all* for his mother, nor will his mother be *all* for him. He will never again be what she is presumed to desire: a phallus. There will no longer be the one, which would mean to be non-differentiated; or the two, which would mean two of the same (the life of the imagination); but most certainly there will be three, the mother's desire being directed elsewhere than onto her child, assuring that difference exists—a condition essential to the development of the human being. This is what is meant when one speaks of the function of the Law and the taboo against incest.

It sometimes happens that we manage to confuse the different domains involved here. Let me give as an example certain medical or bio-medical practices where, through certain medical acts to the human body (operations,[13] medication and institutionalization[14]) it is tempting to raise knowledge to the status of Law. How is it possible, really, that the administration of medication which acts on the brain allows the insane person to enter or to re-enter the realm of the Symbolic? This is a physical act, a bodily intervention which would replace the act of human speech, and which attempts to maintain the relationship to the Symbolic, fragile as it is for certain people.

Permit me to give another example of confusing the different domains: after the tragedy, some men said they had "always dreamed of doing that." What I have just explained casts light on this: it is precisely in this "dream" where the entire difference between the Imaginary and what is Real takes shape. Obviously it is in bad taste to make this known publicly—of this, there is no doubt. But to take exception to the "dreams" of others and to censor them leads exactly to the opposite of what is to be hoped for. It is not the dreams and the fantasies[15] which are dangerous, it is their absence, or the automatic blocking of the word in its symbolic function. Certainly it is this which is most difficult to bear among all the positions possible to identify with—that of the victims, that of the witnesses, that of the parents of the victims, that of the mother of Marc Lépine. Inevitably, this tragedy insinuated itself in the personal lives of those who analyzed it, only to be taken up in numerous discussions between these analysts—it was in a woman's home where I heard this marked identification with Marc Lépine. All this to say that we must not confuse the psychological concepts of masculine and feminine with masculine and feminine biological or sociological concepts.

It is not difficult to imagine that Marc Lépine had what Pierre Legendre would call a fault of *filiation*,[16] a dis-affiliation. Indeed, how can we not recognize in his attempt to join the Armed Forces—which he did under his real name, Gamil Rodrigue Gharbi, the name with which he would have registered his social existence, but which he did not use—a request for recognition addressed to the Father.[17] The subsequent rejection he found unbearable. It is therefore not surprising that he spoke of Denis Lortie* in his letter. Lortie stands for the one who attacks the Referent, desperately

---

* *Corporal Denis Lortie armed himself with a sub-machine gun and entered the Quebec National Assembly. It took several hours to disarm him and secure the release of all hostages.*

attempting to establish himself as Subject.[18] But if Lortie was, in the end, to stand before justice, Lépine could only bring his act to its logical conclusion by having it end in his own death. A woman patient posed this question the day after the event: "Why didn't he start by killing himself instead of killing fourteen women before realizing that it was something inside himself that was not right?" Here is why he could not: Marc Lépine's insane act was directed at *jouissance*,[19] which we are all supposed to say "no" to, and that is why, beyond the tragedy for those who are personally affected by the loss of a dear one, this act is intolerable. While it is part of Marc Lépine's personal life story, it also touches each and every one of us in our own life story, causing us to *imagine* once again that there is a way to thumb our noses at castration and the Law, thus awakening—to be once again painfully re-examined and processed—all that always remains of our grief over our separation from the Mother's body, and showing us both the mortal outcome of its failure and the mortal result of transgressing it. This is how, collectively, it thrusts us into question at the foot of social Order.

Marc Lépine accomplished what is for all of us both desirable and taboo: incest and murder.

Notes

1. In its time dimension.

2. I make reference here to Jacques Lacan's definitions of the Symbolic, the Imaginary and what is Real.

3. I borrow this wording from François Peraldi, who employed this metaphor at a seminar at the University of Montreal on January 16, 1990.

4. This is typical of a certain kind of suicidal reasoning.

5. We will know nothing, either, of the defective role played by repression.

6. Cf. the myth of the primitive horde in S. Freud's *Totem et Tabou* (PBP, 1965).

7. *La Presse*, December 8, 1989, page A-3. See also *The Gazette* of December 7, 1989 where Eric Chavarie attests to this.

8. The scene of parental coitus, imagined or real. This pertinent "vision" emerged from a discussion with colleagues.

9. Some people reported they had been afraid they would learn it was their son who had done this.

10. Literally, that which is inviolable.

11. *Les Formations de l'inconscient*, a review by J.B. Pontalis, in the *Bulletin de la psychologie*, 1958.

12. Meaning he or she who does not yet speak.

13. Too many medical acts such as mastectomies, hysterectomies and cesarians are carried out. It is not a matter of questioning the acute necessity of such interventions, but rather of questioning the abuse of them.

14. For these last two interventions, I am referring primarily to those who are said to be mentally ill.

15. Even though children may well confuse them at times with reality, which can lead to anguish.

16. Cf. Pierre Legendre's *Le Crime du caporal Lortie. Traité sur le père*, Fayard, 1989.

17. Or to the paternal office.

18. Pierre Legendre, op. cit.

19. A *jouissance* which has no relationship to any notion of sexual pleasure or orgasm.

That They Not Be Forgotten . . .

Maria De Koninck and Diane Lamoureux

This letter appeared in Quebec City's **Le Soleil** *on December 15, 1990.*

Women are far from being protected in our society, regardless of what the Human Rights charters say. Judicial treatment of violence against women shows us that the right to protection, surely a fundamental human right, is far from guaranteed in our daily lives. Quite the opposite is true. The unprecedented violence unleashed against the women students at the Polytechnique makes us fear the worst.

As feminists, we are concerned not only because our movement was singled out by the murderer as the source of his problems, but also because this movement is held responsible for social change that is brought about too rapidly.

Yet feminists have proceeded along perfectly normal political paths in this democratic society, and there is really no comparison to be made with the violent act which took place at the Polytechnique.

It must be understood here that an erroneous analysis of feminist achievements is more the result of a tendency to push resistance to change into the background and to underestimate the extent of this resistance, than the result of the rapidity with which changes have come about. Here again, the effect of this rhetoric, which would have one believe that everything has been accomplished (along with its echo—feminism is dead because it is obsolete), is more than illusory. Resistance to the change is, unfortunately, very present. If it does not always manifest itself in the form of violence, it is nonetheless dangerous to deny it.

Our reaction as university professors takes place on two levels. The first one is related to what the university represents, and what the December 6 killings mean in this context. The university is indeed a place where one can learn the kinds of skills and acquire the knowledge which leads to a certain position in society. That this milieu is becoming more and more accessible would indicate that society itself is in transition. Opening the university to women does not simply mean that women will have access to professions previously reserved for men, but that an improved sharing between the sexes in their orientation toward the citizenry as a whole is expected to develop gradually. The choice of the site is no coincidence. *It gives meaning to the act.* The university is one of the bastions of resistance toward women. In this regard, the presence of women in universities implies real social transformation.

The university also makes a place for the confrontation of ideas, in the form of the written and spoken word. The freedom so dear to academics refers to the existence of freedom of expression within a given community. In Quebec, the university has historically played an important role in maintaining this freedom. When polemics are replaced by arms inside the university enclave, there is reason to question the health of a democracy in a given society. In this regard, we hope to see university professors come to the defense of the debate as a means of resolving social conflicts.

Finally, as citizens, we are reacting against violence as an increasingly common form of communication. Regardless of how extreme the act in question, it is nonetheless a *coherent* part of the nature of everyday violence, of which women are the primary victims. We refer to the violence of poverty, psychological violence, and domestic and sexual violence. Ordinary sexism, integrated into everyday life, contributes in turn to its ordinariness. Widespread distribution of images of women in pornographic products nurtures a vision of the world in which women are not only held up to ridicule but physically abused.

The young women murdered at the Polytechnique were refused the right to exist. They didn't give their lives, their lives were taken from them: there was, therefore, a crime against humanity. Yet to us has fallen the task of explaining what is self-evident in this tragedy: the rejection of the underlying logic in the killer's demented act. We must work toward bringing about a society in which women have the right to exist, without creating supplementary victims. Our determination to change this still-misogynist society has been reinforced, and we will apply ourselves even more, in order that such an event never take place again.

Violence, Fear and Feminism: Fragments of Reflection

Simone Landry

Ten days after the event I, who knew none of the Polytechnique women students personally—though I saw their faces in the newspapers and in the chapel of rest at the University of Montreal—still wake up before morning filled with anguish from bad dreams I cannot remember, dreams I don't want to remember. My heart and soul are filled with other people's words, and with my own words: public words, private words, women's words, men's words. To make sense of chaos and non/sense, to go beyond violence and fear—that is what I, like so many others, have tried to write since the sixth of December 1989.

Violence.

The increasing violence in our societies, and violence against women. These two have been placed in opposition to each other since the sixth of December, as if they were two different things and not two aspects of the same reality.

Let's begin with the biological argument, the one that claims the aggressive impulse is stronger in boys than in girls. Nothing absolutely clear has been demonstrated about this argument. Is there really an innate difference, or is there a learned difference? The anthropological work of Margaret Mead[1] demonstrates how extremely important socialization is in the development of aggressive tendencies: the so-called primitive peoples differ enormously among themselves with respect to the emergence of such tendencies, whether in women or men. Some cultures are distinctly more aggressive, others are remarkably gentle and harmonious. As for me, I think that we all have this aggressive tendency, the source and the motor of all action, and that individual differences are much more important than sexual differences. I also think that the socialization process has, for a long time (and it continues today) taken upon itself to stifle any manifestation of this urge in girls, for better or for worse. Whether this urge is because of exuberance and the desire to take control of their own environment, or an expression of their anger, girls have been taught to repress it and to turn it inward against themselves. The opposite is true for

119

boys, who can climb trees, play around with toy weapons that shoot off sparks like real ones, and fight physically with each other without fear of punishment. There is no point in belabouring this—it is common knowledge. What is astonishing is that it is so easily forgotten, and that we feel the need to resort to theories of genetics and biology in order to explain men's unbelievably great violence. This violence is a result of the socialization process that prepares them to be each other's rivals, to take their place in the domination hierarchies built for them and by them, to violently knock out of the running those who would try to get ahead of them, to "objectify" others. Also, it prepares them to disdain and violate, sexually or otherwise, those women who are there to provide for the expression of their sexual fantasies and to give them offspring, those women who belong to them and who do not have the right to exist in their own right, but only to the extent that they conform to this "biological" destiny. One of the subversive effects of this system is that it can only function if men learn how to simultaneously deny their suffering and their emotions, to stifle in themselves that other urge that would allow them to develop consideration and compassion for others.

The asocial nature of contemporary occidental societies is reflected in the disintegration of all value systems and in the disappearance of all great modern ideologies which, until recently, allowed for a certain balance to be maintained. The beacons which, to a certain extent, helped contain the violence in this system with its primary goals of control, domination and power, have disappeared in the general disintegration. Instead we have control of nature in all its aspects, to the point of total destruction of the environment; domination of all those who are an integral part of actualizing this grandiose picture; and a euphoric sensation of omnipotence stemming from the acquisition of power over others. What will become of those who cannot make it in this system, those who cannot hope for the tiniest piece of this much sought-after power and who are incapable of expressing the slightest emotion—those who are also incapable of getting a woman? They look for release. They give themselves delusions of grandeur. I will never forget the image of that young skinhead, on *Le Point* and on *Match de la vie*, who said the following: "When you have a knife at someone's throat, then you feel powerful." Violence, power and fear. I am afraid. Since the sixth of December, I have been more afraid than ever. I'm afraid for myself, I'm afraid for my daughters. Like a lot of women, I have gone through certain phobias in my life. Televised violence makes me shudder. Pornographic violence fills me with horror. Violent acts of sexual aggression, mutilations, the murder of little girls and women of all ages, I find incredibly depressing. Not to mention violence done to children of both sexes, or to old men and old women. The violence that occurs when men settle accounts I find less disturbing—that's part of their game. My daughters, young as they are, have already encountered their first exhibitionist, their first constraints on sexuality, their first experience of verbal violence. They already know the rules of the game—they are not afraid of the skinheads in the Metro, because "they're not after girls, Mum." The "skins" have appropriated the macho law of protecting the weak, i.e. the women. Unlike the male students and professors at the Polytechnique, who were afraid and who had reason to be.

Fear is a normal and understandable reaction where there is danger. Fear initiates a state of alertness which allows us to protect ourselves against the danger in our immediate environment. But is it normal and understandable that half of humanity must live in a nearly constant state of fear because of attacks that could come from the other half? All men are not potential rapists or attackers—I could not subscribe to such a stereotyped image. But nor can I walk down the street or in the Metro with a man walking behind me, without being in a state of alarm, clutching my handbag tight against me, ready to run if need be . . .

Fear, and more fear—men's fear now. Men don't yet have the right to be afraid. We accused the men at Polytechnique of not protecting their "sisters," of not attempting to bring down the killer. And it was from other men, their colleagues, their friends, that I heard this reproach. Boys and men are supposed to control their fear. They're supposed to be "fearless and flawless" knights. Crying is forbidden, fear is forbidden, but violence is permitted. Where does men's fear go then? Unexpressed, inexpressible, it turns into raging anger. What are men afraid of? Who are men afraid of? Like us, they are normally afraid of anything that threatens them, including, when they are little, the fear of all-powerful parents. They are also understandably afraid of aggressive fathers, who they later identify with and whose violent behaviour they integrate into their lives and imitate. They are also afraid of women. Women perceived on an archetypal and mythical level appear dangerous and threatening to them.[2] As members of the most oppressed group on earth, women appear even more frightening. In domination relationships, the dominator is generally afraid of the person he dominates, especially when he realizes, more or less consciously, that the people he dominates do not feel the domination is justified. He is even more afraid when these people have recourse to what Elizabeth Janeway calls "the power of the weak,"[3] which is, on one hand, skepticism before the definition of reality their dominators impose on them, and on the other hand a re-visioning which enables them to validate their own perceptions, develop a new vision of the world, and contemplate concerted action with a view to changing the existing order. Like all oppressed groups who intend to break away from domination by others, feminists of all eras and all descriptions work away at this. If men find women frightening, it is easy to see how they find feminists even more so.

Feminism.

Feminism is frightening. Feminist theory, research and action now permeate the entire social fabric. Some changes are now obligatory. And it is this fundamental criticism of the current social order, at a moment when its subversive ramifications multiply, that entails a most violent reaction against feminism and against feminists.

Feminism calls into question this system, which cannot function without us continuing to take our assigned place. Each time a woman steps out of line and into a better place, she helps to undermine the very underpinnings of the system. The fact that we are capable of being chief executive officers, policewomen, engineers, union leaders, doctors, chiefs of State, firewomen, lawyers, etc. demonstrates that there is no so-called natural weakness in women that would make us inadequate for the positions. Each time a woman plants herself in front of a man who intends to beat her and orders him to show respect, each time a woman slips out from under a man's control, each time a woman chooses independence and self-affirmation over madness, sickness, or suicide, she ducks the image of a weak, dependent, incompetent and helpless victim—the image the patriarchal system requires, if it is to survive.

Marc Lépine got along well with women he considered his inferiors. He showed himself to be kind and generous with the neighbour he "cruised" now and again. But he could not tolerate women who dared to make their way in the world of men, who took the place of men. Thousands of women experience daily the same hostility, misogyny and anti-feminism, which is manifested in a multitude of attitudes and behaviour, ranging from a subtle put-down to indecent remarks. For many of us, this palpable hostility and the ostracism which often accompanies it have led us into complete silence. It has led us to no longer speak of our feminist knowledge of how life and society is organized except in closed circles, to no longer write of it except in specialized reviews and journals which the majority of our male colleagues never read.

Though some outspoken feminists were included in Marc Lépine's hit list, most of the women he singled out were simply women for whom the feminist struggle had opened doors to a particular number of male strongholds. The same thing goes for his victims. They are not dead simply because they were women. They are dead because they had entered into men's sacred territory, and they believed themselves to be equal there. This is what forms the basis for saying that their murders were not only a sexist crime, but definitely an anti-feminist crime. Didn't the murderer say so himself?

The patriarchal system falls apart when we refuse to be mothers, mistresses, servants, or outlets for the repressed anger and violence which the system itself generates and must siphon off somewhere. But the system is also falling apart as we near the end of the century, under the weight of its own contradictions and the death cells which cling to its very roots. Feminism puts forward an analysis which emerges only through a radical critique of this system. If there is an increase in anti-feminism at the present time, it is no doubt precisely because the mechanisms of self-control are gradually disappearing, and the system is getting itself caught up more and more in a series of uncontrollable reactionary loops. Just before the fall of an empire, there is always a resurgence of hate and repression.

Women constitute one of the forces likely to contribute to the non-violent transformation of the patriarchal system. What is more, this transformation will not be able to take place unless women play a central part. As the primary care-givers and bearers of compassion, values that were left to them because they were perceived as being insignificant,[4] women must continue to assume their place in all spheres of human activity. Their presence alone can ensure a gradual change. Without such change we, and our planet, will disappear. It is also essential that we who define ourselves as feminists continue our actions and our theoretical analysis of the patriarchal system in which we live, as well as our analysis of its multiple ramifications in our lives. We must continue to help and to comfort the victims of this system, those who are hassled, attacked, assaulted. We must continue to mourn the dead and to insert ourselves into every environment where women are excluded, including the higher levels of power. We must continue to clear the path for sisters and daughters who, like the young women at the Polytechnique, will assume their right to be there without a second thought and without bitterness. We must continue to rethink the world and to speak out until we are properly heard.

The fourteen women who died on December six will quite possibly enable many of us to once again take up the feminist struggle lost somewhere along a detour in the 1980s. It may enable us to express once again our vision of a more egalitarian world—more harmonious, less competitive and less violent. A happier world, perhaps?[5]

Notes

1. In this text, I draw upon Marilyn French's important work *Beyond Power* (French edition, translated by Hélène Ouvrard, *La Fascination du pouvoir*, Acropole, Paris, 1985), which addresses the work of Margaret Mead. *Beyond Power* is an extremely well-documented theoretical work, which attempts to explain not only the origins and the evolution of patriarchy, but its effect on the evolution of societies to the present day. It is a valuable tool to help us understand what is happening, without separating violence against women from the general violence to be found in all societies at the end of this century.

2. The literature on this subject supplies innumerable examples, and this phenomenon is well-analyzed by Eugène Entriquez in *De la horde à l'État*, Gallimard, Paris, 1983.

3. In *Powers of the Weak*, Knopf, New York, 1980.

4. Cf. Carol Gilligan's *In a Different Voice*, Harvard University Press, Cambridge, 1982.

5. This kind of thinking does not happen in isolation. During the Fall my colleague and friend Armande Saint-Jean and I taught a course entitled *Feminist Research in Communication*. Our many discussions greatly enriched my reflection, as did her work *Pour en finir avec le patriarcat*, Primeur, Montreal, 1983.

Accommodating Profound Social Change

Marie Lavigne, President of the Council on the Status of Women

This text was published in La Gazette des femmes in the March/April 1990 edition.

One of the most painful blows Quebec has ever experienced is now just a few days into our past. Because a band-aid for this wound was needed as quickly as possible, some people tried to explain the act as an individual's isolated gesture. Others, accustomed to dealing with hundreds of violent acts in their workplace as much as in their private lives, saw the act as symbolic of the situation of women in our society. Still others attributed it to a rejection of what women have become.

The pain was too excruciating for hundreds of women and men, and the careful examination of our individual and collective attitudes about violence in general and violence against women was too profound for us to be content with the response of behavioural science specialists. But should reflection and suffering lead us to make this tragedy symbolic of the relationship between men and women in our society?

That would be to suggest that the progress made by Quebec women during this past century—the access to education, better salaries, acquisition of political and legal rights, sharing of household tasks, assertion of control over their bodies and their pregnancies—was all done in an atmosphere of violence. It would also be suggesting that thousands of men are against these changes. To be sure, for the past hundred years women have had to arm themselves with patience in order to disarm the resistance and be perceived as subjects in their own right—to be more than mothers in a family. Women's history has proceeded in stages, in the context of difficult discussions and respect for choice. At times, it has proceeded only after extensive negotiation.

For several generations now, women have lifted barriers one after the other. They now have access to salaried jobs, access to education, growing participation in the mechanics of decision-making, greater visibility in the media, access to various services, etc. Our society is progressively adapting to legal equality. In any case, our occidental societies have no choice in the matter—it would be unthinkable that these societies be deprived of the half of "human capital" women represent. Democracy is such that it *must* include the women.

Support for the egalitarian point of view is part of our present day society. But let us not delude ourselves— real equality is far from having been accomplished. The women who have been confronted with these social transformations have reacted with a form of superpositioning: to the old values and roles, which were those of the home, they *added* those of the world formerly reserved for men. A reciprocal consciousness has barely begun to see the light of day. Social, economic, political, domestic and family life is still organized as if women and men belonged to two distinct groups, as if the interaction of the traditional domains of men and women were but a passing phase.

However, these profound social transformations cannot be ignored. Not only do these changes entail the burden of a double workload for women, they also create tensions between women and men—who are often ill-prepared to face the new realities.

In order that these changes be accommodated, certain things must be done. We are all of us, women and men, in this together. It is unbelievable that women, who form half the work force, earn only 60% of what men earn; that childcare services are deplorably underdeveloped; that employment legislation does not permit parents to coordinate their parental responsibilities with those of their work; and that having children entails a substantial outlay of revenue for a given family. It is also a matter of inadequate public planning on the part of our health system to imagine that women should be able to maintain the care of the household when they have just come out of hospital, or when they must accommodate an elderly relative in the home. As individuals, we must become responsible and call into question our tolerance for violence. We must cease building walls between ourselves where mutual respect is found wanting.

The status of women has been profoundly altered, leaving in its wake a trail of upsets in the traditional relationship between men and women. Not all of us have successfully accommodated these upsets, as the gunfire at the Polytechnique so tragically reminds us. The challenge before us now is to pass from equality on paper to actual equality. The challenge is to construct a society in which every individual accepts that women are full-fledged human beings, equal not only in words or on paper, but equal every day, everywhere and at all times.

The Stone Age

(Letter to the F.R.A.P.P.E.* team)

This letter was published in Le Devoir on December 15, 1989.

Jeanne d'Arc Jutras

About your plea that all violence be stopped forever: your prayers remain unanswered.

It is truly scandalous that since December 6, that horrible day when fourteen women university students were killed on the mountain, still more women have been killed here in Canada, land of our ancestors. This fact sends me crashing into despair.

Here is the news today, December 11: One mother (sixty-five years old) and her daughter were found dead, strangled in their home at New Carlisle. A young woman was found stabbed to death, at the end of a pier at Lavaltrie. Another young woman was shot at point-blank range in her home. Seriously wounded, she will live. Site: Montreal North.

From the moment of our birth to our last second, the killing of women continues, and is increasing. It is not greater gun control, nor prayers, nor pious hopes that will eliminate those who are sworn to uphold the law.

*   *Femmes regroupées pour l'accessibilité aux pourvoirs politique et économique (Women united for accessibility to political and economic power)*

There is no magic formula. There is no fairy godmother and no magic prince. There are no monsters. There are only human beings. Enough is enough, and yet it's not enough.

An isolated act, you say! Begone! Why it's the Modern Stone Age, Madam.

*This letter was published in the **Montreal Mirror**, on December 14, 1989*

An Incitement to Violence

Paula Sypnowich

The mass murder at the University of Montreal marked a macabre close to the "Decade of Women." The response of many men and women has made me wonder if a century would be time enough for us.

Over the past few days we have been repeatedly told that the slaughter was the isolated act of a psychopath, a deranged product of what is, admittedly, an increasingly violent society, but a rare aberration nonetheless. Certainly the culture which produced Marc Lépine is disturbingly trigger happy. The day after the massacre, when the entire city was said to be in mourning, there was ample evidence of that.

A young boy at my local corner store exclaimed, "Wow, cool!" to his friends when he saw the front page photo of a blood-spattered female corpse. Older boys were determinedly shooting animated targets at the video arcade. From a building, identifiable only by the cannons at its entrance and a sign above it, came the sound of gunshots. Regular militia training was going on, as usual.

We learned that Marc Lépine was not the madman we had assumed, had even wanted, him to be. It soon became apparent that the most remarkable thing about Lépine before he executed 14 women was the fact that he was quite unremarkable. Those who knew him described him as "average." The most damning characterization of him is hardly extraordinary—an alienated young man with a history of bad relationships with women, a penchant for war movies, and an abusive father.

But far more important than the unexceptional character of the criminal is the unexceptional nature of his crime. As horrible as the massacre at the Polytechnique was, the response it evoked in many women was not unfamiliar. If the murders bear no relevance to the everyday lives of women in Montreal, why have so many women reacted with fear now that Lépine is dead and gone? Because his act was a condensed version of the same old shit.

It is true that most mass murders are not directed specifically at women. It is also true that most serial murders are. And while such acts of violence against women are still relatively rare, there are others which are commonplace.

By the year's end there will be more than one thousand rapes reported in Montreal, and more than four thousand cases of wife battering. It is estimated that 300,000 women in Quebec are assaulted by their partners, and a woman is raped in Canada every seventeen minutes. That means that when you read this issue, more than six hundred Canadian women will have been raped since Lépine's killing spree. Violent manifestations of misogyny are an everyday occurrence, and the fear of being victimized is part of every woman's life.

Feminists have supposedly made enough gains that physical violence against women is no longer explicitly condoned. But almost every aspect of popular culture implicitly encourages it. At some point the distinction between deviance and norm becomes disturbingly blurred, and the extent to which each can be deranged is only a difference in degree, not kind. The "excitement" induced by caged women in heavy metal music videos, the "humour" found in humiliating women in most comedy, or the "thrill" of watching another woman hunted down in horror flicks is as normal as it is sick.

Feminists are not deriving any self-righteous satisfaction from the political nature of Lépine's act. We would have happily endured without such gruesome vindication. But the significance of Lépine's hatred should be no less obvious than if he had shot into a synagogue.

I do not wish to understate the tragedy of the deaths of those fourteen women. But I mourn their deaths as I do the deaths of relatively anonymous women who are raped and murdered, or as I would if Lépine had gunned down fourteen strippers, bag ladies, or secretaries instead of fourteen aspiring engineers. And I'll end up heartsick again when misogyny is no longer "topical," and the media once again address women's issues only through articles on daycare subsidies and debate over who does the dishes.

The Vicious Circle of Violence

Gloria Escomel

In moments when we are most fervently in need of hope, we often find solace in a retrospective vision of history. We tell ourselves that there has been some progress after all: for almost half a century now, since the horror of the two world wars, there have been only regional conflicts with fewer casualties. The global phenomenon of torture is becoming more and more systematically condemned, and this condemnation may have reduced its incidence and forced it into hiding. The death penalty has been suspended in many countries. A number of States have laws which protect human rights. Yes, violence is becoming more and more unacceptable. Then, just when we are ever so slightly reassured a tragedy takes place, very close to home, and its proximity sends perspective out the window.

Seen against the backdrop of other horrors in the world and against the incalculable number of victims of all sorts of violence, what are fourteen unfortunate young women from the Polytechnique who were murdered by a "madman" (as he was quickly labelled, no doubt to further diminish the impact of the crime)? Nothing, I dare say. A mere drop of water in the ocean—but a drop that happened to splash us in the eye, here in this country where we generally have only personal violence, with the exception of some local "gang wars", and where the crime level is relatively low, compared with other countries.

But here is precisely where relativity hits home: this "nothing", these fourteen lives, fourteen destinies brutally interrupted, put us in mind of the millions of other destinies cruelly mowed down by global violence. Victims cease to be abstractions and figures. In any case, it is not the extent of a massacre that shocks us, it is the injustice. The media has made us so attendant on figures! Three thousand dead in one confrontation, seven thousand dead in a war, fifty people dead in a particular railway accident, six million in a genocide.

They use figures to attract our interest and arouse our pity. Is this not true? Why, news that a man was killed by a drunk friend, or a woman murdered by the man she lives with, barely gets a raised eyebrow when we read the paper. That is, of course, unless they are our close friends or relatives.

But for all women, these fourteen particular women *are* our friends and relatives. Astounded, we recognize them as are our sisters—yes, victims who stand as symbols of us all. More so than women who are killed here and there, one by one, in a war, or at the hands of their life partner? Quite possibly, for this crime was signed "I hate feminists!"

This battle cry has come to rest in our memory. Every day, during the brief time that we find ourselves in an "enlightened" milieu, we try to forget that feminists are hated, ridiculed, reduced to powerlessness. Yet every day hundreds of hateful, hurtful and more or less startling actions and comments are directed toward feminists and women. No one says anything and they appear to be unimportant, commonplace.

From the time that feminists first raised their voices to speak of this as a political crime—violence against women in general—it was said they exaggerated their case, that they didn't know how to conduct themselves, that they only wanted to start up the "war of the sexes" once again, that they were"co-opting" the tragedy for their own purposes. From that moment on, efforts were made to silence them, and with remarkable unanimity.

The Polytechnique massacre has cast a particularly brutal light on all latent misogyny. It has revived feminist anger and pain, and shown to a great many men (and women) that feminist claims and analyses are still legitimate. Some men, who were themselves prepared to state that feminists were using the tragedy to gain political ground, were so horrified by the reaction of their male colleagues that they were shocked into acknowledging that their natural acceptance of equal rights is not something shared by all. Others, who had been considered progressive, shouted that feminists were taking shameful advantage of the tragedy.

But what does "taking advantage" mean with such an event, and in this context where feminists were targeted by name, if not the very basic need to reflect upon a hatred directed at ourselves. By way of opposition, they put up the argument that the murderer was an isolated individual. Are we denying then that the individual is capable of making a political statement? But what could still be left to interpretation the day after the tragedy takes on a completely different perspective two months later. The public debate which followed the tragedy demonstrated beyond a doubt that a great many men hate feminists. I'm not talking only about those men who wrote articles, gave interviews, or swamped the open line shows, but also about those who, in ordinary conversations, expressed their contempt for feminists and feminism. The gunman killed fourteen women, but in his wake thousands of men symbolically killed all feminists.

Is this what the politicians, men and women, wanted to avoid when they hastened to interpret Marc Lépine's action as that of a madman? Did we hasten to make this look like an ordinary killing in order to ensure that, upon close examination of who the victims actually were, no spark of hate would cause a fire to break out, inciting all latent and repressed hatred to run rampant in the full light of day?

Crazy or not, Lépine symbolizes a particular hatred: he is, therefore, not so isolated as all that. Feminists understood this immediately. But that is what terrified so many men as well, men who dreaded that they might *ipso facto* be accused. And it is what frightened the many women who worried that the war of the sexes might have flared up again, and it is what infuriated men who did not like to see male violence being named the culprit. It is what made so many others feel ashamed, honest men who acknowledged it in themselves, and in others like them. And it is also, in the end, what finally gave the event an aura of scandal, which forced us to think very seriously about it indeed.

Because by all official counts feminism seems to have come to nothing (which is one way to say they haven't come to grips with it), we are now told we're in the postfeminism era, as if the problem were solved. And we are now being coaxed toward the big reconciliation—forgive them, they didn't know what they were doing—as if contemporary men were not like men before them at all! We are also being told that "the oppression of women" was quite a big word, wasn't it, and anyway, ancient history these days. They say that everything possible has been done for women, who have simply to reach out and take what is rightfully theirs, and if they don't take it, well, then they didn't really want it in the first place. Obviously, for all those men, and women too—for we cannot overlook those reactionary and colonized women who believe they've achieved equality with men, by stepping on other women just as men have done—the only way they could save face and continue to profit from their soothing and demobilizing discourse was to propagate the notion of a solitary crazy killer and a feminist milking of the tragedy.

But for those women whose conscience tells them that, despite certain undeniable gains, women on the whole have taken only a few little steps, and only on the condition that they show their pass; for all those women who have understood that feminism is still the only instrument that will move us forward with respect to equal rights and changes in attitude; for all those women, the tragedy at the Polytechnique, and especially the public debate which followed, have unfortunately merely confirmed their analyses.

And now what are we to do? How can we continue to support this slow progress others are still able to call combat—though there has been neither rifle fire nor the death of men, and the only violence has been verbal?

First of all, undo or sever the complex knot of diversified violence, this knot of fear and cowardice which is strangling us, a knot that will hang us if we aren't careful. What I mean is, we have to look the situation straight in the face, stop looking for phony escape routes, accept that hatred, contempt, and even irony are difficult to bear and that they can destroy us.

Then we must tell ourselves that at all levels violence is a serious and contagious disease, and that we have to loosen its grip on us. Violence is essentially masculine, let's face it, and it attacks not only women, but, in most cases, anyone who is weaker. I have said "essentially." Because I have had it so often repeated to me that violence is part of the essence of man! But when we look things squarely in the face, we know very well that a woman can have the potential for violence just as a man can. With one important difference: it is men who exercise this potential. When we state that 82% of murderers are men, we are also stating that 18% are women. And every one of us knows that we also experience the urge to fight or to kill.

But violence is admired among men, and is part of their upbringing, while among women it is repressed. Since these influences are so powerful, why not raise men the way we are raised: that is, brought up to condemn violence, brutality, and destruction? We seem to be doing the reverse: preparing women to join the army! A long process of de-conditioning should at least result in a controlling instinct, similar to that which women have learned. No, women's liberation will not come through imitating men, but rather through abandoning certain specifically male values and, yes, imitating women.

Then, all those demented brute force tributaries in our society—wrestling matches, violent sport, violent films, sadistic pornography, and so on, will begin to lose their appeal.

Working at non-violence seems critical to me. But to accomplish this change of attitude, we will have to work for a very long time. It will take a long time for everybody to understand that feminists who work to abolish patriarchy are working for more than the abolition of masculine privilege—that men are also trapped in such a society. Make them understand. Convince them. Persuade them. Have we done anything else, since the earliest days of the feminist movement? Maybe we have to step up the intensity, confront men anew wherever they are, each one in his own milieu, in all circles, large and small. Violence against women is a problem they don't understand very well, if they mean well. And they understand it only too well, if they don't mean well. It's time they understood, by any means, and I still believe in dialogue.

But it is up to us to understand certain tactics, taken from martial arts, that consist of turning the adversary's force against him.

We have to understand that now is not the time to deny our strength, our analyses, our condemnations, our objectives.

Understand too that there is not one single strategy for accomplishing our objectives, but a thousand, and in this diversity we are strong.

We don't all use the same tools, we don't all have the same negotiators, we don't all come from the same background. We must therefore select different strategies, as a result of this diversity. Men's violence against women, no more than men's violence against other men, will not be reabsorbed overnight. This is why the work we've undertaken must in no way disperse feminist solidarity; if it does, we risk discouraging not only ourselves, but our youth. We would be that much more vulnerable to being co-opted when the different factions are divided, or weakened by doubt.

May it be the case that in this, as in other areas, women disassociate themselves from the patriarchal system which oppresses them, and which oppresses so many men, whether they are conscious of it or not. Our greatest strength is that our actions do not perpetuate, even in the legitimacy of our cause, the power imbalances we are seeking to destroy.

Yes to Feminism, No to Feminists

Micheline Dumont

Since the sixth of December, the word FEMINIST has shown up everywhere in the media, ranging in meaning from a condemnation (condemned to death, literally) to a proclamation. Between these two poles, the real nature of feminism has been overlooked—for it is true that, most often, feminism is ignored. Be that as it may, I wish to look at the ways in which History has tried to accommodate this important social movement.

The word feminism is about a hundred years old. It is thought to have been used for the first time by Hubertine Auclert in 1882 in a letter to a women's rights activist.[1] It is important to note that this word was applied to a movement whose theoretical origins could be traced back to the end of the eighteenth century, and whose first political organization formed around 1848. A women's rights movement has existed for a century and a half, despite the fact that most official accounts of history ignored this. The movement spread throughout the majority of occidental countries from the 1890s onward, and it gave rise to a network of national and international organizations, next to which present day feminism pales in comparison. The English suffragettes initiated at the beginning of the century—and this without government subsidies—a core group of eighty people who were paid to work for the cause of women's suffrage.[2] The French feminists published a daily newspaper, *La Fronde*, from 1897 to 1903 to publicize their principal demands.[3] Other examples abound.

Of note, this feminism, from the moment it first appeared, provoked virulent reactions on the part of several groups of men, which contributed to establishing a dichotomy between GOOD and BAD feminism. If contemporary detractors of feminism were to read the feminist texts of that era, they would no doubt be dumbfounded by the reasonableness and the timidity of the demands found in what was called BAD feminism. As for the GOOD feminism, it had already been co-opted by the religious and political authorities in order to give it a definition that would keep women connected to the private sphere, and in the context of family responsibilities. Women themselves supported this definition of GOOD feminism. To establish a distinction between several types of feminism is therefore not particularly original: it's a phenomenon that dates back a hundred years, and it is nothing more than a rudimentary strategy to divide the forces of protest. But let us continue.

Feminism, it appears, became lethargic not long after the First World War, after women were granted the right to vote. But this statement doesn't stand up to careful examination. Indeed, the collective mobilization of French women was considerable between 1920 and 1940, on the issues of votes for women, contraception, legislation and education.[4] American women, from 1925 on, began the long struggle for the Equal Rights Amendment, and they established powerful women's associations. And the Québécoises began, against all expectations, to demand the right to vote in provincial elections.

After the disruption caused by the Second World War and the period of social conservatism which followed, it took women some years to point out the profound inequalities of a social system which exploited their competence both in the home and at their paid job outside it. New circumstances, brought about by the gains of the earlier feminists, called for a new analysis. The word feminism, which had been set aside, came back into use to once again put a name to this complex concurrence of women's demands. "Women's liberation, Year Zero!" wrote the French feminists in 1970; they were apparently ignorant of the feminism which had gone before.

Over the past nearly thirty years in Quebec, since 1961, new demands have been drawn up.[5]

In 1966, the Québécoises endowed themselves with powerful organizations, such as the FFQ and the AFEAS. Since 1969, the women of all of Canada, in the context of a very official and very upright Royal Commission of Enquiry, took the measure of their subordination and became aware of their problematic situation.

Young women twenty years ago, those who thought feminism unnecessary, out of date, old politics, and so on, experienced a most acute oppression. In all the leftist political movements where they were active as people in their own rights, or so they believed, in the interests of all egalitarian, pacifist, nationalist, socialist causes, they came up against a domination: the men in the movement dominated the women. This experience was to give rise to a more radical analysis of women's situation, an analysis which finally resulted in avoiding the pitfalls of equality.

The good old dichotomy method of the Nineteenth Century was back in fashion: this time, there were MODERATE feminists and RADICAL feminists. The very "daring" demands of the BAD feminists of the Nineteenth Century reappeared on the slates of the so-called MODERATES. And in a society which considered itself egalitarian, the demands of the RADICAL feminists turned everything upside down. The situation they were protesting was so intolerable . . . that they, the radical feminists, were judged intolerant.

But a strange phenomenon happened at the end of the 1970s. One by one, radical feminist analysis came to reinforce the demands of moderate women. It became more and more difficult to categorize the issues. So much so that at the end of that decade, the dividing line between the MODERATES and the RADICALS had become less and less obvious. Little by little, all of feminism came to be considered RADICAL.[6] But in spite of everything, women's issues were documented, serious, level-headed, and politicized. It was no longer possible to brush them aside. It was no longer possible to laugh at them, as had happened in the House of Commons, when the problem of battered women caused members to burst out laughing, thus inciting women's general indignation.

Nothing is more disturbing than reading documents about the condition of women. And if reading these documents makes one ill at ease, one must inevitably ask oneself the reason for this uneasiness. It is not the document that is aggressive; it's the situation that is intolerable. In ancient Egypt, the Pharaoh executed the bearers of bad news. Today, we choose to blame those who protest against them. A new dichotomy has come to separate feminists: those who can be talked to (REASONABLE WOMEN) and those who are scolds (FAULTFINDERS). It is no longer feminism that is being judged, but those who document and describe feminist demands, those who persist in keeping the issues before the public. For women's situation is far from being resolved; on this, everyone is agreed. Let us acknowledge that the REASONABLE WOMEN are those nobody needs to reason with: they don't discuss it; they say, "I'm not a feminist." This is rather convenient for those who claim to speak from masculine objectivity; they have only to give the impression of understanding it all and explaining it all. But what to do about those FAULTFINDERS, those women who put forward an interpretation which disrupts the beautifully masculine syllogisms (which, incidentally, many women have taken up)? What to do about those who insist on bringing it up? You are hurting your own cause, people keep saying to them, that's enough now. Be quiet.[7]

We can also easily make the statement that it is now FEMINISTS set up in opposition to FEMINISM. Now that women's analyses have been recognized as legitimate (even the bishops have taken a position on family violence!), it would be very much appreciated if the women would finally be quiet. The tragedy at the Polytechnique has provided us with a lovely example of censorship and self-censorship. Messers Dubuc, Leclerc and Bourgault* were able to speak about it: they were applauded! But women ought to be quiet about it; what they have to say doesn't interest anyone. They are guilty of speaking out. They are even guilty of violence against men with fragile psyches, as Mr. Marcel Adam** explained! But Messers Dubuc, Leclerc, and Bourgault hastened to speak of other things.

Be quiet—as if that doesn't just make you sick. It reminds me of that German film on domestic violence: *Women's Silence Makes Men Strong.*

Notes

1. K. Offen, "Defining Feminism" in *Signs*, Vol.14. No.1, 1988, pp.118-157

2. M. Vicinus, "Tactiques des suffragettes anglaises: espace des hommes et corps des femmes" in *Stratégies des femmes*, Tierce, 1984, p.408

3. D. Armogathe, *Histoire du féminisme français*, Des Femmes, Paris, 1982, p. 371

4. H. Bouchardeau, *Pas d'histoire les femmes!*, 1978

5. *Le Devoir*, feature edition of June 25, 1961

6. L. Noël, "Haro sur les féministes!" in *Liberté*.

7. P. Bourgault, "L'avenir est aux femmes" in *Châtelaine*, May 1986

*   progressive Quebec journalists
** editorialist

MINISTRY AND MAGISTRATURE

This is an excerpt of a text
which was published in Le
Devoir December 20,

Changing Things Around

Paul Chamberland

We are in danger. We are in a state of war. Who, us? What do you mean, "us?" The December 6 massacre was aimed at women. We will never be able to fully comprehend the meaning of this act of rage, for feminism involves so much more than what this act took aim at. The stakes involve much more than the struggle of women for equality and dignity.

The ethics of violence to which we now openly adhere is an unchanging male ethics which has existed unimpeded since the beginning of the patriarchal order. It demonstrates on a global scale the murderous excess by which a resolute force is able to savagely defend its supremacy against whatever seriously opposes it.

With women, it is the essential power of the feminine which comes to be threatened: harmony, compassion, the intelligence of the heart. Threatened above all is the masculine/feminine dynamic composition, the "us" which alone has the ability to determine within each individual the conditions of his or her achievement. This "us," reinforced by solidarity and nourished by generosity, is composed of women and men determined to act in a manner which impeaches the harm done by the lords, their violence and their reign. Above all, it brings about a feminine ethics.

This "us," we must emphasize, is the power of women: from it is formed the active hearth, a distinguishing power. But even as we recognize its distinguising characteristic, we must also see in its emergence a call for men who acknowledge feminine ethics to rally round and commit themselves without reservation to the radical transformation these ethics entail. Yes, it is urgent to change things around. It is a matter of life or death. And in this matter, the steadfast assurance of love is most certainly required.

If we are to be on the side of the "living" we must be vital men, we must be "intelligent beings" with women. Feminine ethics has been formulated, by Quebec feminists among others, as a *gynecology*. The expression is profoundly appropriate, for today the Earth is also in danger. Rambo's knife is in Gaia's breast—it is plunged deep into the heart, here, now, and everywhere. Gaia is our mother, our sister, our daughter, our companion, our equal. Our realm.

＊

All Men are Guilty

This is an excerpt of a text published in **Le Devoir** *on December 12, 1989.*

Dorval Brunelle

Before our indignation can be appeased, before the horror which is re-enacted on a daily basis gives way to a protective numbness, we must wade through the explanations.

The motives and causes which pushed one brain completely off the track one afternoon in December must be situated in the larger context of principles and values which sustain us. From this perspective we are all guilty, we men, to the extent that we tolerate a deepening ambivalence at the heart of our societies, about women. At the level of image we deck our women with flags, adulate and venerate them, yet in our violent personal lives we strike, humiliate and murder them.

The veil which covered our brutality and our aggression has been torn beyond the comfort of words and intellect, beyond the progress of institutions and theories. In the twenty-five years since 1964—the year the killer was born—Quebec women have gained equality piecemeal. Even so, it has had to be extracted under extremely trying conditions. At the same time, we men have been taking part in the unfurling of increasingly intolerable, systemic violence towards women. The statistics on criminality, domestic violence and the economic status of single mothers confirm this.

Never before in history have women been placed in such a precarious position. Not only have men become torturers, they have become so cynical that they systematically duck out on their responsibilities as fathers, husbands and partners.

Feminists have every right to rise up. All these crimes are political in nature and this last one, the one at the Polytechnique, supremely so. It is not good enough—it is not good enough *anymore*—to see psychological or pathological crimes in men's constant and incessant resorting to violence. The extent of the phenomenon, its universality, ought to lead us to conclude there is evidence of collective tragedy.

The assessment is clear and the proof of it is borne out by experience. The way things stand now, men are incapable of instituting equality between the sexes. What they give with one hand in charters or laws, they swiftly take away with the other when they desecrate certain values and destroy lives.

Today, we murder our daughters. To be able to put words to this horror, we must begin by making a commitment to fight all kinds of discrimination, from the most intolerable to the most insignificant or petty. In the meantime, we have forfeited the right to regard women with righteousness.

Where Are the 49% When We Need Them?

Greta Hofmann Nemiroff

Discovery and Hope

I am a fifty-two year old woman, and an educator. For the past twenty years I have been researching, writing and teaching women's studies. Like most educated women of my generation, I am certified to practice Men's Studies—in my case the literature written by, about and for men. I was thirty years old before I grasped that all the learning for which I had been validated depended upon my satisfactorily learning men's "official version" of their reality. It was only then that I understood my experience was excluded from the very subject matter which I had so assiduously studied.

Like many other feminists of my generation, I was deeply influenced by the liberation and anti-war movements of the 1960s. Since I was a university teacher at the time, I lived my feminism by co-teaching the first Women's Studies course offered in a Canadian university. Those were heady times—each work of research, each insight and each publication was actively discussed among women as we explored the vast uncharted continent of our own experience. Hundreds of women attended our classes, often expressing a desire to make some sense out of their history and their lives.

We would discuss sex roles, sex role stereotyping, women and work, sexuality and sexual proclivity, nature versus nurture, reproduction, mothering, the family, women and education, women and love, and the psychology of women.

We did not talk about women and violence.

The words "sexual harassment" and "wife battering" did not yet exist in 1970. Men were certainly not about to coin them. Rape, incest and other forms of childhood sexual abuse had not yet risen from our collective unconscious to public articulation. We spoke generally of cultural misogyny, but it was some time before we made the connection that misogyny was systemic and frequently translated itself into violent action against women.

As explorers we were optimistic that if we could gather sufficiently convincing statistics, men would understand the error of their ways and share the world equally with us. After all, historically it was they who had precipitated numerous bloody revolutions in the name of equality.

There were usually a few men in our classes, but they were never more than 10% of the group. Some of them came to laugh or be fussed over, but most came to learn and deepen their understanding of women. We spent an inordinate amount of time raising their consciousness.

Since then violence has become slowly unveiled. While the media produced hopeful works portraying feisty and ingenious women in non-traditional jobs, pornography was being exposed, discussed and related to widespread misogyny and increasing acts of violence against women. These exposures did not suppress the public penchant for violence against women. Such violence may be portrayed in vignettes of sadism in porno magazines and films; it may be manifested by the suicidal impulses of some men to kill their wives, their children and themselves. We have seen it in a rash of gang rapes in universities. In response to these phenomena, women's groups have increasingly appealed to legislators for changes in laws related to violence against women.

As we busily worked on briefs and in front-line women's groups, many feminists were fueled by optimism that the world could change through our labours. When legislation did not seem to deter sexual harassment, sexual assault or the battering of women and children, we redoubled our efforts. We helped draft new laws, we instituted more courses in self-defense, we hopefully planned for our daughters to learn to think, to defend and to fight for themselves.

We reasoned that men would eventually value sharing the world equally with women and shedding their burdensome machismo. They would join us in creating an equal society. We knew that there had never been a ruling class which voted itself out of power. We knew that some men would resist the empowerment of women. However, we reasoned that as women became more qualified and active in the public sphere, patriarchy would wither and drop off the vine.

Twenty Years Later

Last night there was a massacre at the University of Montreal. We can think of nothing else. This morning I am interviewed on TV. Another guest on the program, a rather prominent lawyer, accuses me of exaggerating when I observe that the killer was a misogynist. "There is no proof of that," he says pompously, "You are jumping to conclusions." "What about the selection of victims?" I respond,

"What about Lépine's remarks about feminists? What about the hit list in his letter?" I try to sound reasonable, not like the "crazy lady" his eyes reflect back to me.

Later that day, the young women in my class cry: "They were such great girls...all so smart and ready to be engineers. I can't bear it," one girl weeps. Another tells us: "I couldn't look at my boyfriend this morning, even though I know it's not his fault." We talk of our feelings and make plans to attend the vigil after class.

The young men are silent in class. What does their silence mean, I ask. One of the most gentle, a quiet young man, suddenly bolts to his full height—well over six feet. Pounding a fist into the palm of his other hand, he shouts: "I've never been violent to a woman in my life." I believe him, comprehending that the young men are silenced by a sense of guilt by association. To turn their guilt into action, I ask: "What're you going to do about it, then?"

More silence. Then they ask what I think they should be doing. "You have to stand up and be counted," I say, today, tomorrow...always." They are respectful and indicate they will be more sensitive to woman-hating among their peers.

However, only the girls attend the vigil.

That night I cannot sleep; I am having an imaginary talk with all the young men in the world. I tell them this:

Lately women have been concentrating on ourselves. We have not been as devoted to dispensing "civilizing" services to the society as we did in the past. We have even learned how to appropriate some time and resources for ourselves. We naively thought you would change alongside us. We did not understand that male culture offers you very little self-esteem other than the approbation of other men and, at the very least, the subjugation of women. It is only by helping yourselves that you can help us.

The next time it happens, please refuse to laugh at sexist jokes. Speak up against each injustice you see or hear about, even if it means risking the anger and violence of other men. It seems that everyone is afraid of violent men, even other men.

Rehabilitate male culture and cleanse it of gratuitous violence.

You are the best people to talk to young boys. Help them gain self-esteem through collaboration, through sharing, and through gentleness. It takes courage to refuse to be violent, to resist the pressures of violent men.

Some people will treat you like they treat women, making disparaging remarks about your sexuality. Learn to transcend such foolishness.

Above all, form close friendships with other men and share your experiences, for you understand one another best. Dare to show your love for other men, for women, for children and—ultimately—for this wonderful planet we share.

About Schools

Marc Lépine spent more of his life in school than in any other institution. Ultimately he passed through two community colleges in his unsuccessful bid for a diploma. It appears that most of his teachers in high school and CEGEP do not remember him. There is no record of his requiring or taking psychological tests. He is best remembered by the salesmen dressed as soldiers of fortune at the store where he liked to drop in to chat about guns and where he may have bought the murder weapon. Although he was not considered in any way extraordinary, they remembered him. His best friend was shocked by the murder. He recalled frequent misogynistic remarks from Marc, but he simply never took them seriously. It is normal in our society for some men to make sexist remarks and others to accept them as the norm. Within male culture, verbal abuse of women is not generally regarded as either noteworthy or pathological.

Teachers are not clairvoyants. We cannot prognosticate who will break down or who will murder. However, we do have an obligation to offer our students a curriculum of possibility: the notion that there can and should be a better world. The values underlying the post-secondary curriculum have neither been examined nor changed over the past half century. Most of it is still grounded in male bias and tradition. While there are Women's Studies courses in most post-secondary institutions in Quebec, their clientele is mainly self-selecting and female. Clearly notions of gender fairness and sexual equality are *not* reaching those most in need of exposure to these ideas.

Educators must take the time to consider what and how we teach and to identify our gender biases. We must have the courage to become learners as we investigate models for gender-fair curriculum. Male teachers must join women as agents of change to ensure a safe and life enhancing society. By overtly discussing sexism and violence against women, and by publicly abdicating the privileges of superior force, male educators can model appropriate behaviours for men.

Unless men commit themselves to changing male culture, violence against women will continue with their passive collusion, their uncomfortable silence and nervous laughter. Without their recognition and renunciation of the power of silent collusion, our society has no hope of honestly honouring the victims of the December massacre, those vibrant young women prepared to contribute to their society on new and radical terms.

This is an excerpt from a letter published in Le Devoir December 19, 1989.

The Church and Women

G. Decelles

At the funeral of the fourteen young women, murdered by someone whose suffering assumed the shape of anti-feminism, there were dozens and dozens of men who dominated the ceremony. I experienced this massive masculine presence at the altar as absurdly extraneous. It was a despicably ostentatious display of profound sexism in an institution which considers itself in the process of moving toward liberation.

This is unfathomable tragedy: the young man, in a moment of imbalance, while committing an unstable act, separated the boys from the girls. The Church, in its ceremonies, solemnly does this very thing itself. Its unchanging structure does it as well, accompanied by bizarre historical rationalizations.

It speaks a religious rhetoric that claims to promote women and men in society. Yet, within the Church, a contradiction the size of a cathedral: the status of men is entirely different from that of women. Women are equal with men before God; however, the sacerdotal rituals, a fundamental element of ecclesiastical life, are reserved for children of the male sex. This alone constitutes an insult to female identity.

When one knows to what extent the Church's sacerdotal functions lead to participation in the Church hierarchy, to its administration and the power elite which affects its orientation, trying to make us believe that these "role differences" are congruent with "equal status for women" is a thoroughly repugnant insult to the human intellect.

As for me, I have long since redirected my research and spiritual life into less dogmatically sexist environments. But so many people I care for still cling to this religious faith which cruelly dashes my every hope with its flagrant contradictions. Will there one day be a massive get-together of Christians who will open themselves to hearing what the Holy Spirit must surely— through so many of these horrific events—be crying out to them?

But this conversion to Equality would call for yet another conversion, which would be a miracle, and one which I no longer believe will happen: the Church would have to develop a healthy democratic nature, rather than wield dogmatic power. It would have to establish a climate where research into meaning would hold sway over what is forbidden.

In my opinion, the sign will come from somewhere else. Life makes its way where it finds an opening.

Anachronism

Anne Savary

This letter appeared in Le Devoir December 19, 1989.

I attended the funeral service for the Polytechnique murder victims . . . on TV. These victims, all women, were targeted by the rifleman who wanted, he said, to have revenge on feminism, which he felt was ruining his life as a man.

While observing the religious ceremony, I couldn't help noticing in front of the altar one of the more powerful symbols of the male monarchy which still permeates our modern society.

All those men—there were about thirty of them gathered around, priests, bishops, archbishops—were still perpetuating the absurd myth that women cannot assume the same responsibilities as men, for reasons which continue to remain obscure.

Such a symbol, engraved in the farthest reaches of our consciousness, runs at cross purposes to the ideal that those young women had chosen for themselves.

This is an excerpt of a letter published in Le Devoir *on January 3, 1990.*

I am a Protestant

Michel Despland

I am a Protestant who is familiar with ecumenicalism. I have at times participated in Catholic worship. This time, it really was not possible. For I believe that if people need priests, there ought to be some of both sexes. The Protestant in me, before the moving demonstrations of grief channeled through the gestures of the Catholic faith, could have kept this conviction hidden deep inside, out of respect. But not so my mother's son, my sister's brother, my wife's husband, the father of my daughter.

On reading your homily, I shared your sorrow. But I felt yet another sorrow: nowhere did you admit—or even let it be understood—that there is a conflict in our society with regard to women and their aspirations. In my field of work, there is a great clash of ideas on the subject of women, and conflicting attitudes toward them. Is this not the case in yours?

In any case, since you see no problem, you haven't indicated any possible solutions. Perhaps it's time to bring back the old slogan: if you are not part of the solution, you are part of the problem.

Ministers of the Gospel must proceed with caution, but they cannot, in the name of Love, refuse indefinitely to come to a decision, when faced with unjust practices and angry protests.

In Quebec, there isn't yet a strong enough secular tradition to give rise to a national gathering of people which would emphasize unity rather than "partisanship". I sincerely regret that in the first phase of the tragedy which has befallen us, we were not able to participate in a ceremony where all human beings were on an equal footing.

Genealogy

Louise Bonnier

The source of our grief and our fear, in which can be found our exclusion from the social system, is slowly revealed to us during these days of wrath and indignation.

The gunman, a sinister symbol, holds office in the public square. He separates the men from the women, eliminates the women. Out of sight, denied, veiled, that's what we are for the masculine upper chamber, which, a few days later, will carry out the mechanics of religious ritual.

Be there, or do not be there. Be there and chance being rudely rebuked; do not be there and let this false neutrality, which is really male power, say what it wants. And now, this: being there could signify taking the place of those crushed in the competitive system.

A replica of a man wants revenge and looks for a scapegoat. He prepares a list of women whom he considers defiant, just by being where he would like to be.

It seems that the official perspective, by nature patriarchal, is incapable of comprehending the straightforward meaning a feminist analysis gives the facts, and in the days following the massacre we collectively experience the destructive effects of sexism.

Paralyzed, we watch the media search for meaning, where the commentator obliterates the simple evidence that it was truly a criminal murder of women whose "feminist" intention to be in a forbidden place was strongly resented.

And then, after this too vulgar denial, there were the various adjustments of *focus*, which either exaggerated or diminished the gunman's act.

Projected into the macrocosm where all violence is equal, the sexless gunman hides his hatred of society in choosing "by chance" a female target. From this perspective, the commentator piously condemns all forms of violence, and the most important, the most fundamental—the form of violence that makes all the others possible—slips out of sight, obscured by silence.

Conversely, the commentator anxiously questions a team of experts who trace the family history that made such a deranged act possible. Why the son and not the daughter? Why is the father, rather than the mother, the carrier of violence? It would never occur to the commentator to think of this. He is content for awhile to ruminate on the shortcomings of maternal love, but eventually he resorts to the consequences of the breakdown of the family.

This gunman talks, writes, accuses: he has conscientiously decided who is to be at fault—all women whose presence he cannot bear, and whose audacity to want to move in circles of knowledge and power means he would have to make others atone for it. Regardless of the commentator's attempts to co-opt the incident and make violence seem like an everyday fact of life, the following anathema makes the rounds: feminism as a latent defect, feminism as a wrong to be eradicated. When it comes to paying the price for stepping into public life, one woman is as good as another.

When and how was the gunman able to develop this wild and vengeful association? This question opens up innumerable paths of reflection, as the first days of grief elapse. Gradually, it begins to weigh on our collective women's consciousness.

This anathema, indispensable factor in the mechanism that drives the killer toward his victims—*he didn't invent it*—is a free agent in right-thinking rhetoric, sometimes a bad joke, a nail file, a scarecrow. It functions as a diversion, keeping women who would want to change things diverted from conscious awareness. At the same time it points out, to those who would advocate revenge, the dreaded loss of false privilege. One example among many: I have in mind a caricatured scene — two enormous women fighters beating up on a tiny Jean Doré,* demanding their Chantal Daigle** Boulevard!

It will be said that the gunman, a long-time community college student, was forced to put up with radical feminist rhetoric, in the face of which a number of male students felt put down, felt they were made to look insignificant, and subsequently were outraged. Was this "victim of feminist oppression" simply settling his accounts, having been pressured into his role as aggressor by all those acting in collusion to exaggerate the ill effects of sexism?

After the abominable killings, we heard this version of the facts: demagogic feminism, using all means available, locks men into sterile guilt: at best, men are cynical; at worst, violent.

Our beautiful francophone and Catholic province, with its "happy are those who suffer . . . ," stayed silent. And what about

* *Mayor of Montreal*
** *see note page 68*

this sophism, its secular counterpart: "life goes on", offered to us *ad nauseum* between the commentators' moments of stunned silence.

All this is highly likely: that the gunman found himself in contact with a generalized condemnation of violence against women; that he was confronted with his status as objective oppressor and anxious to deny it. Likewise, when I analyze in class Susan Brownmiller's prescriptive ideas about rape, and we come to the passage where she states that all men terrorize all women, I have noticed over the course of years that male students experience the same surprise and have the same difficulty with this statement: men, having penises, can, during wars and riots, and pressured by collective emulation, be forced to rape. Whatever my pedagogical concerns about sorting out the levels of involvement such a statement must entail, there is inevitably, at that moment, a shock—the extent of which, and the consequences of which, would be difficult to measure.

It is an indisputable fact that feminism makes men feel guilty collectively and individually. People wanted to direct this guilt onto feminism itself, and in so doing practically embraced the gunman's very madness, at a time when our sensibility as women—potential targets—had us piercing the cold indifference of those who hold the power. All this had us precariously perched in unreality and helplessness.

We were like Jews, or Armenians, told that past exterminations hadn't taken place. We were also the girls and women for whom incest and rape had been a longstanding private reality, and for which acts we were supposed to feel guilty.

This psychological violence, which consists of blaming the oppression on those who are subject to it, while accusing them of "provoking" it because they have protested against it, accusing them of "profiteering," because they attempt to establish the relationship between the various mutilations (recriminalization of abortion, pornographic violence, and other marvels of our Judeo-Christian world)—this psychological violence has been present in our conversations, meetings, meals, workplace, everywhere. The killings caused those who spoke to us to feel ill at ease and to withdraw. Some were even able to go so far as to term our exacerbated sensitivity slightly "hysterical," hoping that the storm would wear itself out. Let's talk about something else, they seemed to say, sometimes a little impatiently, but always paternalistically.

No, definitely, the ramifications of such a shock are so great that I am reclaiming the old slogan "I remember."* I am going to place it above the portraits of these sad characters who represent three generations of cannibals, dismemberers, and women eaters.

First of all there is the "predicator," who, blinded by a stereotyped formal language, postpones until the afterlife the solution to our exclusion from society. A fatalist, close to fanaticism and fundamentalism, a disturbing leftover in this fin-de-siècle, he looks completely innocent, almost quaint. I am able to nevertheless measure the extent of his power when those who criticize him straightaway lose their jobs; I bother to take the influence of his sermon into account when I hear the clarion sound of federal government amendments to the abortion law. He wants a more "restrictive" definition of the health issue, which would exclude all the cases presented on the bases of social, economic, and psychological factors. In any case, the adjective "psychological" ought to disappear for good; they've already conceded, after much hesitation, that women have souls: let's not ask for more than they can give.

The predicator insists on two written medical opinions regarding the state of the mother's health. He would like to see restoration of the traditional waiting period between the request for an abortion and the act. But he really hopes to instill doubt in fragile and impulsive beings by penalizing not only those who undergo an abortion, but those who perform them. Come to think of it, the predicator is an important character I must never lose track of.

My second portrait is that of the commentator. This character appears more relaxed; always a good democrat, ready to let others speak, self-effacing, polite, lacklustre and grey, he sinks his claws into my brain, always unexpectedly, with his book of media tricks.

He possesses powerful instruments for creating change, extraordinary means with which to educate. The "performance society" which pulls the strings has unfortunately ordered him the voyeurism-exhibitionism combo medium rare. Last night (February 7, 1990) he outdid himself: I was allowed to learn which sort of knife a certain guru, who calls himself Moïse,** used to amputate the arm of one of his women ex-followers, as a form of punishment for some kind of sin. I was taken aback by his apparent incredulity, his eyes

---

*   *the motto of the province of Quebec*
**   *Moses*

that were popping out of his head. It made me think of Jean-Luc Mongrain* with Corporal Lortie.**

This second portrait is particularly significant for me. The commentator and I are more or less the same age. From early on, we were similarly lectured by the predicator; we went to separate schools together, boys in one, girls in the other. Gradually, the commentator saw the masculine bastions taken by storm—at least that's how he most often remembers it—by a few women.

After having applauded this novel event, which cost the weird old predicator dearly, the commentator began to find the situation less amusing. As he grows older liberalism has its limits. He has to conjugate grammar to make room for the Other, experience things viscerally, feel fear and anger on a gut level. He realizes this, strangely enough, after having offered his condolences to too many people—he goes so far as to offer them to the killer posthumously—and with this slip of the tongue, he walks away from the incident unharmed, turning the page of the "news-in-brief."

He would definitely have to change. But at his age, digesting twenty years of feminism is a lot to ask of him, when he has only just begun to enjoy the comforts he so rightly deserves. Not to mention that he finds feminism has a ring similar to puritanism and fanaticism, in the sense of castration, frigidity, provocation, and so on. No doubt, also something of what's left of bad old jokes. A good boy nevertheless, he promises to look at the question some other time, when he has more time. Alas, he knows very well that time devoted to reflection these days is becoming more and more rare.

Let's move on to the last portrait. A worthy heir, the gunman armed with a phallic weapon—fourteen targets in twenty-eight minutes—is looking for me. His eyes are strangely vacant: a computer screen shimmering, alone in the dark of night. I am waiting for facts to appear on the screen, facts that only an investigation of the acts and deeds of the killer could give me. It seems unrealistic, for the moment, to expect this kind of information; it would surely lead to a full-scale social issue, and that is what we are supposed to avoid.

I am therefore unable to complete this portrait, which disturbs me enormously, for I risk coming face to face with the killer at any moment, without even knowing it.

*   *host of a popular talk show*
** *see note page 114*

I read somewhere that it is now possible to train fighter pilots with computer programs; the difference between the training lab and the first flight would be insignificant. Wading through the statistics on the numbers of permits to carry weapons and the weapons themselves—models, dimensions, how they operate—I am trying to find the coefficient that articulates the relationship between the ideal level of insensitivity to other people's pain—women or other mammals—and the mass of stimulation required if one is to manage to pull the trigger.

Our Daughters, Ourselves

This article was published in **The Globe and Mail**, *December 8th, 1989*

Stevie Cameron

They are so precious to us, our daughters. When they are born, we see their futures as unlimited and as they grow and learn, we try so hard to protect them: This is how we cross the street, hold my hand, wear your boots, don't talk to strangers, run to the neighbours if a man tries to get you in his car.

We tell our bright, shining girls that they can be any-thing: firefighters, doctors, policewomen, lawyers, scientists, soldiers, athletes, artists. What we don't tell them, yet, is how hard it will be. Maybe, we say to ourselves, by the time they're older it will be easier for them than it was for us.

But as they grow and learn, with aching hearts we have to start dealing with their bewilderment about injustice. Why do the boys get the best gyms, the best equipment and the best times on the field? Most of the school sports budget? Why does football matter more than gymnastics? Why are most of the teachers women and most of the principals men? Why do the boys make more money at their part-time jobs than we do?

And as they grow and learn we have to go on trying to protect them: We'll pick you up at the subway, we'll fetch you from the movie, stay with the group, make sure the parents drive you home from babysitting, don't walk across the park alone, lock the house if we're not there.

It's not fair, they say. Boys can walk where they want, come in when they want, work where they want. Not really, we say; boys get attacked too. But boys are not targets for men the way girls are so girls have to be more careful.

They plan for college and university and with won-der and pride we see them competing with the boys for spaces in engineering schools, medical schools, law schools, business schools.

We bite back the cautions that we feel we should give them; maybe by the time they've graduated things will have changed, we say to ourselves.

And then with aching hearts we take our precious daughters to lunch and listen to them talk about their friends: the one who was beaten by her boyfriend and then shunned by his friends when she asked for help from the dean, the one who was attacked in the parking lot, the one who gets obscene and threatening calls from a boy in the residence, the one who gets raped on a date, the one who was mocked by the male students in the public meeting.

They tell us about the sexism they're discovering in the adult world at university. Women professors who can't get jobs, who can't get tenure. Male professors who cannot comprehend women's stony silence after sexist jokes. An administration that only pays lip service to women's issues and refuses to accept the reality of physical danger to women on campus.

They tell us they're talking among themselves about how men are demanding rights over unborn children; it's not old dinosaurs who go to court to prevent a woman's abortion, it's young men. It's young men, they say with disbelief, their own generation, their own buddies with good educations, from "nice" families, who are abusive.

What can we say to our bright and shining daughters? How can we tell them how much we hurt to see them developing the same scars we've carried? How much we wanted it to be different for them? It's all about power, we say to them. Sharing power is not easy for anyone and men do not find it easy to share among themselves, much less with a group of equally talented, able women.

Now our daughters have been shocked to the core, as we all have, by the violence in Montreal. They hear the women were separated from the men and meticulously slaughtered by a man who blamed his troubles on feminists. They ask themselves why nobody was able to help the terrified women, to somehow stop the hunter as he roamed the engineering building.

So now our daughters are truly frightened and it makes their mothers furious that they are frightened. They survived all the childhood dangers, they were careful as we trained them to be, they worked hard. Anything was possible and our daughters proved it. And now they are more scared than they were when they were little girls.

Fourteen of our bright and shining daughters won places in engineering schools, doing things we, their mothers, only dreamed of. That we lost them has broken our hearts; what is worse, is that we are not surprised.

At the Polytechnique

Andrée Stanislas-Cyr

Letter to M. Courville, director of the Polytechnique, published in Le Devoir, December 18, 1989.

My daughter, who is a student at your school, missed the gunfire by two or three minutes. I understand how disturbing all of this must be for you, and I appreciate the fairness of your decision with respect to postponing the exams, providing support to young students, and so on.

This notwithstanding, I feel the need to share with you certain feelings I experienced after the tragedy. I wish to broach the subject of actual instances of misogyny which exist in your school, perhaps more there than in other areas of our society.

It is my hope that these horrifying events oblige all those who were involved in misogynous acts, women or men, to acknowledge that it is time to put an end to such outright contempt.

Whether it is:

— a professor who speaks to his class as though it were composed entirely of male students;

— films shown at the Polytechnique which show only stereotyped images of women, which do not correspond at all to your female students, and which contribute to even greater ambiguity in women's relationship to men, within the very walls of your institution;

— the strip-teases that entertained the graduates at their graduation parties (I'm trying to guess what the women graduates must have felt in this not-so-distant era). This mentality, alas, has not disappeared over the space of a few years; if anything, it perpetuates itself. Surely, this cannot be denied.

— the necessity for each woman who has the courage to enter your world to adapt to an environment which does not share her values.

The only way to survive this is to stop being tolerant, and even lax, toward this solidly rooted behaviour.

I support your position in favour of more women in your profession. It might be a good idea to keep implementing this policy until 50% of engineering students are women.

Equality in the profession would then be more obvious, and the profession, as you yourself have emphasized, would only be better for it.

Take Nothing for Granted

Micheline Bouchard

On December 6, 1989, I am presiding over a benefit dinner for *La Fondation Jeunesse 2000*, an organization dedicated to improving the situation of young people in our society. After thanking the donors for their generosity, I stress the importance of helping young people who are dealing with violence, poverty, and drug problems. A little while earlier on the news, I learned about the murders which took place at Montreal's school of engineering, the Polytechnique.

When I speak to the audience, I dare to suggest that we can avoid this kind of tragedy, if young people who are having a difficult time could have the chance to develop their self-confidence and secure their independence. At the same time as I make this plea for young people, from twenty to twenty-five years of age, deep inside I am furious that a young man so violently attacked women engineering students. This act is especially painful for me because it was directed against women, particularly young women who had chosen to invest in a profession where they are still largely under-represented, and because in doing this, he has defiled the place where I was a student twenty-five years earlier—and even that long ago there was no discrimination. I still believe women have the right to become engineers. I am also convinced of the fundamental role of young people in the society we are in the process of becoming. However, the tragedy which has just taken place at the Polytechnique brutally reminds me that we still have a long way to go before the two groups fully assume their respective roles.

Despite the individual nature of this act, it is nevertheless indicative of existing values in our society. Unfortunately, prejudices toward the place and the role of women still exist. Does this mean the profession is not open to women? No, that is not the case. On the contrary, engineering is probably one of the few professions which knew how to welcome with pride the small number of women who joined their ranks, in the university as well as in the work force. Women engineers who entered the work force more than ten years ago may have been exposed, more than their young male colleagues, to sexist situations, but we who went before relentlessly pushed back the barricades for those who were to follow. The question is not whether there is a place for women in the profession, but rather what society must do in order to eliminate the prejudices which cause young girls to hesitate before choosing this career.

If the murderer thought he was contributing to the elimination of women in engineering, he failed miserably. The opposite is happening. The entire engineering community, men and women engineers, male and female engineering students, have joined forces in order to demonstrate to the world that this insane act will not inhibit the future entry of girls into the engineering faculty. This mobilization was eloquently displayed at the victims' funeral. Some two hundred and fifty women engineers, and an impressive number of women engineering students, wore white scarves around their necks, symbolizing their sadness and their sympathy for the victims' families and friends. Many male colleagues were also present at the funeral. We were all deeply pained at having lost some of our own to a violent death. The entire profession was plunged into grief. We felt a deep need to come together, and to take action, in order that their deaths not be in vain.

As for me, I had a chance to act very early on. On the same night of the tragedy, after the benefit dinner, I contacted a personal friend, engineer and director of Public Relations at the Polytechnique, Michèle Thibodeau-De Guire. She had just heard the horrible news. I offered to help, and throughout the course of the next days' events, I had the opportunity to make myself useful, and to follow through on actions I initiated.

The morning after the tragedy, I was contacted by the media for my comments. This opportunity to express my pain loud and clear was some comfort to me. I suddenly considered myself fortunate to be able to publicly express my state of utter confusion, and also my determination to continue the work of consciousness-raising, to which these young women had contributed. There are so many people who want to do something, make themselves useful, help, comfort someone. Helplessness aggravates their suffering.

I was fortunate in being closely connected to the engineering community and the Polytechnique. Also, I have the means at my disposal to facilitate communication between myself and all those men and women who are able to offer comfort and encouragement.

Another group of engineers spontaneously volunteered to organize the mailing of letters to all women engineers in Quebec, inviting them to attend the funeral in large numbers and, now more than ever, to play their role as models and leaders by wearing the symbolic white scarf.

The Order of Quebec Engineers joined us in this initiative, and several of their administrators gave us their support.

The Polytechnique students' association contacted me, asking me to join in their movement. Likewise, Claudette MacKay-Lassonde, who was the first woman president of Ontario's Professional Engineers Association, offered her assistance in spreading this initiative across Canada, starting with Toronto. We wove a giant support network across the country, which in turn reaffirmed the ties between the engineering students and the men and women graduates already out in the work force. From this newly erected base, various initiatives have been taken. The Polytechnique students' association launched a movement to promote non-violence and greater gun control in Canada. Overseen by Claudette MacKay-Lassonde, a scholarship was created in memory of the victims, dedicated to encouraging the participation of women in engineering. Alain Perreault, the president of the Polytechnique students' association, spontaneously offered to collaborate in setting this up. The Canadian Council of Professional Engineers, which brings together 137,000 of the country's engineers from their constituant associations, participated. The Commemorative Foundation of Canadian Engineering was formed. The Polytechnique itself joined in, creating its own scholarship.

Today, what are we to conclude about the tragedy at the Polytechnique? In the first place, that we can never take anything for granted in our society; that we must continue to promote the kind of respect and equality that will enable women and men to fully contribute to our developing society. Second, that there is enough generosity and good will in this world; we have only to channel it positively.

The victims of the Polytechnique massacre have not died in vain. They have enabled the living strengths of the profession to come together to promote the future mass influx of women into engineering.

The profession will never be the same. We owe to them this turning point in history.

Hunting Rifles?*

Louise Nepveu

Letter published in La Presse December 20, 1989.

The Solicitor General of Canada made the following inappropriate remark following the tragedy at the Polytechnique: when someone buys a car, and he decides to use it for driving into a crowd of people, we don't go around prohibiting the sale of cars. So why prohibit the sale of certain firearms? The answer is hardly difficult: the primary function of a car is to transport people from one place to another, while the primary function of a firearm is to KILL.

Nor is Canada's Justice Minister, who is concerned about not losing the hunters' vote and who is under pressure from firearms merchants, about to prohibit the sale of semi-automatic weapons.

It is up to the population to get organized: harass your member of parliament, write to the newspapers, do everything legally within your power in order that the law on firearms be modified as soon as possible. Semi-automatic weapons *are not* hunting rifles; any experienced hunter will tell you that. The carnage at the Polytechnique would have been infinitely less deadly if the killer had not carried a weapon capable of cutting down so many people in such a short period of time. Obviously, there are other things we can do to halt the spread of violence in our society, but obstructing the sale of murderous weapons is critical and urgent. The society we want for our children is not the one proposed by the Justice Minister of this country.

If the government continues to allow the sale of semi-automatic weapons, its members will have the death of innocent people on their conscience, and they will be future murderers' accomplices, regardless of what they say.

---

*   *Students at the Polytechnique circulated a petition to restrict the sale of semi-automatic firearms.*

The Will to Know

Monique Bosco

Every single one of them starts by saying that if you're going to talk about what happened at the Polytechnique only silence is appropriate, decent, necessary. And then they pick up the microphone, or the pen. Read them. Read them again. They've neglected the most elementary rules of propriety, of rhetoric even. Pell-mell they quote God, Sartre, Hegel, and the Gospel according to Saint Mark (Jean-Paul Desbiens, *La Presse*, December 21, 1989).

I hear Frère Untel* has traded his neighbourhood slang for the garb of a hideous werewolf. Luckily the Inquisition is far away. Otherwise, the "witches" of today, coming under his jurisdiction, wouldn't stand a chance. Such hatred of women! Yes, it's been a long time since I've seen the like of it. Such virulence! Maybe not as far back as Jean Larose's *Petite Noirceur*, but the Big One, the forties and fifties. I'm serious. Duplessis.** Still kicking.

There was also Jean Paré's violent and ideologically confused editorial, "No guilt complex" (*L'Actualité*, February 1990, page 9), where he happily mixed together six of one and half a dozen of another—yellow star of . . . or is it red, no it's pink—refusing all the while "to own" his own stuff. All the same, having achieved some distance, it seems to me that this tragedy must be treated with the intellectual rigour that human catastrophes deserve.

Do you remember Cayatte's 1952 film: *We are all killers*? The great slogan from May 1968: *We are all German Jews*? And what if guilt were to reside in the space between; that is, neither all Jews nor all killers, but lodged somewhere between the guilt of the murderer and the victim's impossible destiny.

So, not all victims and not all guilty, but all human. Unfortunately, too human. Groping around for something, nevertheless—maybe insight, truth, justice.

I called this text "The will to know", after the French title of Michel Foucault's book on the history of sexuality,[1] because I am

---

*   *Frère Untel, or Brother So-and-So is the pseudonym of Jean-Paul Desbiens, a polemicist known for his violent condemnations of "joual" during the 1960s.*
**   *Maurice Duplessis, Premier of Quebec from 1936 to 1939 and 1944 to 1959.*

convinced of the urgent necessity of helping along this "will to know," without which a just society is not possible. Like the Statue of Liberty, democracies must hold high the torch. And the light, why, we have no right to extinguish it, to get in the way of its illuminating all round, under the pretext that neither the sun nor death can look each other in the face.

I swear, if they had planned it, they couldn't have done a better job of turning horror into chaos. The flood of news, often condensed; unfounded rumours; the many points of view and commentaries—ultimately they contributed only to disinformation. Too much information can mean no information at all, or no critical information, by which I mean news supported by fact, not opinions or sentiment. What did they give us? A jumble sale of terrifying images. Witnesses and parents bombarded with idiotic questions. But more on this later.

First of all, I would like to establish loud and clear that we have absolutely no right to "normalize" such a massacre by explaining it as an *isolated* incident, claiming it is only the result of *an individual's* murderous rage, and that it will never happen again because the killer fell by his own sword.

We have no right to squelch this killing with deceitful excuses, so-called indications of compassion and respect for other people's pain. There is often nothing more inhuman than the insensitive sentimentality with which many a horror has been masked. This I learned in the Second World War.

If the December sixth killing is stifled, under the guise of protecting the victims' parents and friends, it is censorship, with its repressive apparatus, that will manage, insidiously, to convince the general public that this was a wise move, that there is a certain propriety to be observed in such cases, if we wish to continue to "live in peace." There is no shortage of proverbs inciting us to let sleeping dogs lie. Apparently, women were being hushed up left, right, and centre, before they could even get a word out! Measures were taken to determine what women would be allowed to say, and when they were to be quiet, so they wouldn't be improper, hysterical. "Hey, you! Keep your mouth shut."

That men admit to identifying with Marc Lépine, doesn't seem to particularly surprise or shock anybody. But if women struggle to make themselves heard, they are immediately accused of co-opting the situation.

"Women are trying to take advantage of the situation in the interests of feminism." If I've heard that once, I've heard it a thousand times these past few weeks. This is what offends me. I have never been a member of any party, I have never been part of a movement—radical or otherwise—but now, I can say that because of this I've had second thoughts . . .

Isn't public condemnation against women activists motivated precisely by the fact that, when one looks closely, womens' conditions warrant protesting? They are right to be afraid, right to point out that hatred against feminist women is on the rise, that it is getting bigger, this hate; it is directly proportionate to women's conditions improving. Hatred against young women too, who are no longer willing to be silenced, who even enroll in the Polytechnique these days. Cassandra, as far as I know, was never popular with men, and not with her sisters either. And nobody wanted to listen to Cassandra. Not to understand, nor to hear what she had to say. Today, more than ever, we have to tell all—even if, and especially if, doing so conflicts with our emotional and affective security.

We have to acknowledge that steps were taken immediately to make sure that certain truths would never see the light of day.

"You want to know more, do you? Know what? Haven't you learned, seen, heard enough? You want more macabre details, is that it? Shut up, all of you." Silence. Only silence. But I know that the law of silence is the most unjust of all, and that self-censure is dangerous and reprehensible, even in, and especially in, a democracy.

On this eve of 1990, it is ironic just the same that *glasnost* should be possible and desirable only in the East. Let us not forget that historically Quebec has suffered more than enough from repression.

To get back to having the will, or desire, to know, I'd like to quote this passage from Foucault, in the section entitled "The Repressive Hypothesis":

"There is no binary division to be made between what one says and what one does not say; we must try to determine the different ways of not saying such things, how those who can and those who cannot speak of them are distributed, which type of discourse is authorized, or which form of discretion is required in either case. There is not one but many silences, and they are an integral part of the strategies that underlie and permeate discourses."[2]

What discourse, which perspectives, have we heard so far? At the time I am writing, there has been the in-house police report, and the "home-made" reports of the journalists, pointing out—a bit late—that it had taken a little while "longer among the francophones than among the anglophones to clearly emphasize that it was an attack against women, specifically, against feminists." (Gérald Leblanc, *La Presse*, January 12: "The Coverage of the Polytechnique Massacre".)

In the hours that followed we had the privilege of hearing the politicians' points of view, each one as insignificant as the next, and I mean this in the strongest sense of the term: the ones in power, and those in the opposition, simply one-upping each other with platitudes.

We, the people, the so-called articulate individuals, we were waiting. Psychiatrists, psychoanalysts, and a few other "ists" for good measure were invited to every broadcast discussion. Their rhetoric was officially reinforced and set off to advantage; they spoke of childhood, trauma, the absence of the father. What do I know about that?

And then, the catharsis. The chapel of rest, the solemn funeral at Notre-Dame Cathedral, transmitted by television. "A first class burial," as popular jargon would have it.

I waited. I waited patiently. They let us hear the students' slogan: "Let's stick together." At the risk of offending them, I must say I gritted my teeth in disbelief.

"Let's stick together." It was a bit late to think of that, and to put it in those terms.

Nobody, though, spoke of the non-assistance to people in danger. The entire University, isolated, high up on its mountain, was strangely silent. The cohort of professors afflicted with paralysis. The intellectuals? Mute. Yes, there was total silence in that Babel of words.

I finally understood that comfort could come only from those whose job was to impartially exercise justice. I felt like Kafka's hero, settled in before the door of the Law in his parable, "Before the Law". And it was the word of law, precisely, that was slow to make itself heard. Or rather, which refused to assume its proper role. On December twelfth, one could read in Le Devoir: "The Coroner does not foresee a public inquest into the murders."

So, I had made my decision. Like that rough but determined peasant in the book, I took up residence in front of the door of the Law. I drew up a petition, now signed by hundreds of women, and sent two letters to the Minister of Justice, the first dated December 18, 1989. As of February 4, 1990 I have yet to receive the most rudimentary acknowledgement of receipt.

Since that was likely, and is still likely, to take forever, I tried on my own to find some semblance of response for the unanswered questions I carried with me day after day.

I went back over that fatal sixth of December.

"You didn't see anything at Hiroshima," says the Japanese to the French tourist in the film made by Alain Resnais and Marguerite

Duras. "I saw everything," she tells him. Obstinately, he repeats, "You didn't see anything at Hiroshima."

I too saw everything and nothing that night in December which will haunt our collective memory forever. Chilled with horrible dread, I watched the program *Ce soir* on TV. Nauseated, I refused to accept that another new horror, a new terrorism, now existed. Right here and now, a hostage-taking incident had been successfully carried out by a single armed man.

"Women on one side, men on the other."

"He told us to leave, and we did."

I tried to keep watching, to glean some facts. Everything seemed contradictory and derisive. Journalists, harassing the witnesses, boldly asked in front of the cameras what was on everyone's mind, questioned the parents as to how they were taking the loss, asked about their grief.

I went to bed. I slept. I had nightmares. I got up to vomit. This is no metaphor. I retched as if to rip the soul.

Women get hysterical; everybody knows that. Friends I questioned had also felt on a gut level this mortal blow to themselves and their sisters. Each one felt it right where they had already known fear, shame, helplessness.

Much has been said up to this point about men's dismay. And the women? Surely it wouldn't be expected that women brush this off as though they were not absolutely stricken, as though they did not feel it in their body and in their memory of other carnages carried out against women? I, for the first time in my life, dreamed about Auschwitz.

"Women on one side, men on the other." Yes, Auschwitz is what this brought back for me. The procession towards the crematorium. Today, many generations of students have not had to study history. Shameful. Adults with no knowledge of what has gone before are doubly penalized, and vulnerable.

This is why that very first night when I heard a young woman, a student at the Polytechnique, get angry at the journalists' questions, I knew what she was trying to defend. But I thought she was on the wrong track, for she vehemently declared: "What happened inside is none of *your* concern!" This struck me as evidence that it was not simply a private incident or tragedy. Exactly! We, you, I had a right, and even a duty, to know what had happened in there, what had really happened in there.

It doesn't help to forget (to "try to repress" would be more accurate). The recent past, the horrors of this century, and all those stretching back to the beginning of time, should be proof enough that it doesn't help. We say: "I remember."* But what is it we remember? How many years have to pass before it is considered appropriate to talk about the camps, the gulag, Cambodia, the Korean War, Algeria, the Katyn massacres, Armenia, My Lai, or Oradour?

When on December thirteenth I drew up the petition calling for a public enquiry into the events at the Polytechnique, I provoked a resistance on the part of, among others, the journalists. They insisted, sometimes aggressively, that I explain to them what such a petition could hope to accomplish.

"What are you expecting to gain from this? What do you want to know exactly?" But if I had known what I wanted to know, I wouldn't have needed an enquiry, public or otherwise. That it is deemed necessary for a coroner to carry out a private investigation is already proof there is something that requires investigating.

In demanding this public enquiry with a petition signed by women only, I am trying to show that it was these women who were singled out and put to death. In any other circumstance, I would be in favour of including men, and that, from nursery school onward. But the separation of the sexes that took place that night at the Polytechnique should never be allowed to slip from our collective memory. There was indeed a separation; there was discrimination on the basis of gender.

You will have noticed that in this text I have mentioned the name of Marc Lépine only once. The issue of homicidal madness and rage is too complex, I believe, to be addressed in a single paragraph. It will be sufficient to recall the epigraph of *Thérèse Desqueyroux*, where Mauriac inscribed these words of Baudelaire:

"Lord, have pity, have pity on the insane! Oh, Creator! Is it possible for monsters to exist in the mind of one who knows why they exist, how *they brought themselves into being*, and how they could have done otherwise . . ."

And doesn't this just immediately remind us that guilt is at the heart of the matter. Original sin, if one is a believer, teaches us that we are all guilty. To different degrees, certainly. But to want to believe, or to attempt to persuade us, that there is not a guilt complex to be had here, this is to vainly attempt to erase society's

---

*   *see note page 156*

problem: everyone has rights, but people seem to forget periodically that these rights also entail duties.

To save Captain Dreyfus, at the risk of "dirtying the honour of the French army," Zola wrote *J'accuse*. It cost him a great deal. As for myself, I don't accuse. Today everyone knows very well that honour cannot be saved by lies or silence. It seems to me that the big taboo in this instance is male behaviour with regard to violence. Could it be that men have lost their sense of honour? The question not to ask: "Rodrigue, are you heartless?"

I buried myself in the beautiful literature I love. Let me assure you, there are numerous examples of panic-stricken fear that overwhelm the greatest of heros from Antiquity to the present day.

The *Iliad* overflows with examples of the most courageous Greeks and Trojans seized by panic-stricken fear. They all go through it, one after the other. Here, for example, in Song XVI, is Hector:

"But by now the Trojan withdrawal from the ships had turned into a noisy rout, wild as the onrush through the sky of a storm-cloud from Olympus and the clear heavens above it, when a tempest is unleashed by Zeus. They fled across the Achaean works with their tails between their legs; and as for Hector, he was carried off at a gallop, arms and all, abandoning to their fate such of his men as were perforce detained by the hazards of the trench."[3]

And since the only points of view permitted in the prevailing media *doxa* of these past few weeks were those coloured by psychoanalysis, I went back and re-read Freud. Here is an excerpt from *Group Psychology and the Analysis of the Ego*, from the essay entitled "Two Artificial Groups: the Church and the Army":

"A panic arises if a group of that kind becomes disintegrated. Its characteristics are that none of the orders given by superiors are any longer listened to, and that each individual is only solicitous on his own account, and without any consideration for the rest. The mutual ties have ceased to exist, and a gigantic and senseless fear is set free. At this point, again, the objection will naturally be made that it is rather the other way round; and that the fear has grown so great as to be able to disregard all ties and all feelings of consideration for others. . . . If an individual in panic fear begins to be solicitous only on his own account, he bears witness in so doing to the fact that the emotional ties, which have hitherto made the danger seem small to him, have ceased to exist. Now that he is by himself in facing the danger, he may surely think it greater."[4]

If we wish to avoid similar panic in the future, if we want above all to avoid a fearsome return of repression, then we must continue to make demands, to fight for a public enquiry that will be carried out with all the rigour and fervour worthy of research into the causes which allowed this tragedy to happen the way it did, and not in any other way. Only by means of a thorough investigation will we be able to analyze what actually happened before, during, and after the sixth of December. One would think that the signs of active misogyny, reported in, among others, student newspapers all over Canada, could have been identified months and even years before. It will also be necessary to carefully scrutinize what happened on the night of December 6. This will require a reconstitution as precise and detailed as an archival document, an historical chronicle.

And we must also analyze what happened after December 6. For "the will to know" has no limits. More than an enquiry, I would like to see this become a quest, a quest for truth. And truth is not dangerous or frightening to see, despite the old sayings. Painters have understood this very well; in the hand of the woman rising naked from the well and radiating light, they've always placed a mirror.

Notes

1. Foucault, Michel, *La Volonté de savoir*, Paris, Gallimard. English title: *The History of Sexuality, Volume I: An Introduction*, translated by Robert Hurley, Pantheon Books, New York, 1978. Otherwise known as *The Will to Know*.

2. Ibid. p. 27

3. Homer, *The Iliad*, translated by E.V. Rieu, Penguin Classics, 1983, p. 302

4. Freud, Sigmund, *Group Psychology and the Analysis of the Ego*, translated by James Strachey, Bantam, New York, 1965, p. 36

The Hidden Side of the Mountain*

Catherine Eveillard

I

At first there was nothing.
Then there was a Mountain and a river.
For a very long time
there was only the Mountain and the river.
The Mountain was home to birds, deer, and wolverine.
The river overflowed with fish.
Then the Indians came
and learned the lore of the land.
Much later other men and other women came
on boats the likes of which the river had never seen before.
They built a city.
They cultivated the land, which yielded generously.
The earth was good,
bountiful, and easy to work.
As for the women, they had many children.
These were good women, generous and ardent.
The city now stretched between the river and the Mountain;
soon, it had spread all around.
The Mountain's rocky flanks protected it from men's ardour.
The animals had long since fled,
and the humans decided to bury their dead there.
Meanwhile, the city was paved with asphalt.
The people hurried more and more.
From time to time, with an effort, they lifted their head and each time
they took in the view of the Mountain like a revelation.
It reassured them of their own immortality.

---

* Mont Royal, which the inhabitants of Montreal affectionately call "the Mountain," is situated in the heart of the city. Around it can be found parks, a lake, a residential area, and some buildings of the University of Montreal.

II

And then, one evening, the Mountain moved.
It was in December, just before Christmas.
Everyone was at home in front of the television,
for the world was particularly turbulent at that time.
Fourteen shots rang out through the night, and then one more.
But this was not on television.
This was here, on the Mountain.
We had to wake up.
We cried out, we wept, we insisted the killer be caught: he was
found.
It was a young man who had received a machine-gun for
Christmas.

After all, maybe it was just a game that went bad.
There are so many toys that look like the real thing; it's easy to
make a mistake.

But the Mountain continued to fume,
a bitter smoke that seized one by the throat.
The truth would have to be told.
The fourteen victims, they were all women.
The young man with the machine-gun, he took his own life.

Fourteen, that was a lot. It was humiliating.
The bodies of all those women lay among the other dead
on the Mountain.
Those who survived said they'd been under suspended sentence
since the day they were brought here by boat.
They said that the Mountain alone knew their suffering.
And so it was they buried their dead there,
sang their songs to them there.
They draped the trees with their dreams and the dreams rotted
in the ships' hold.
They said they couldn't take it anymore.
The men swore it would never happen again, and that the death
of those poor girls would not be in vain.
They swore this, and then said Mass,
but that did nothing.
The next day, another woman was killed.
And the day after, yet another one.
The hemorrhage could not be stopped.
Men lost their head.
The women ran away.

The Mountain was red; no one
dared look up at it.
It accused them all.
They felt accused.
They said that only a crazy person would . . . but
how many crazy people were there in the City?
At this rate, we didn't count anymore. Some of them went
unnoticed.
A very large number had to be killed for the morning papers to
talk about it.
It was better not to talk about it.
We lived in cars, behind bullet-proof glass,
one foot on the accelerator.

III

They wanted to prohibit remembering it.
But they couldn't wipe the blood off
the windows of the Polytechnique.
Like live coals, it flared up every evening
at the very moment the University
loomed large
in the shadow of the cemetery.

IV

Later, much later
—but this could be tomorrow—
spring followed the winter which had
lasted several centuries
—but this could have been last winter.
The earth was spongy with water.
It was good land, bountiful and ardent.
That year there were many flowers
flowers the like of which had never been seen before.
Men and women knelt to pick bouquets.
And with each flower they picked,
a woman they had loved came back.

AUTHORS OF TEXTS PREVIOUSLY UNPUBLISHED

Élaine Audet is a writer.

Ginette Bastien is a political consultant on the abortion issue.

Sylvie Bérard is a student of French Studies at the University of Quebec at Montreal.

Louky Bersianik is a writer.

Louise Bonnier teaches Philosophy.

Monique Bosco is a writer and a professor of French Studies at the University of Montreal.

Micheline Bouchard is an engineer.

Marie-Thérèse Bournival is a journalist.

Nicole Brossard is a writer.

Andrée Côté is a lawyer and part-time professor at the University of Quebec at Montreal.

Micheline Dumont is a historian and professor at the University of Sherbrooke.

Gloria Escomel is a journalist.

Catherine Eveillard is an architect; she is presently completing a study of sacred landscapes.

Nicole Lacelle is a freelancer and lesbian feminist activist.

Simone Landry is a psychosociologist and professor in the Department of Communications at the University of Quebec at Montreal.

Andrée Matteau is a psychologist and a sexologist.

Greta Hofmann Nemiroff is a writer-activist and Co-Director of The New School, Dawson College, Montreal.

Renée Ouimet is an acupuncturist.

Monique Panaccio is a psychoanalyst.

Armande Saint-Jean is a journalist and professor in the Department of Communications at the University of Quebec at Montreal.

Marie Savard is a writer.

Text of Marc Lépine's Suicide Letter

Editors' Note:

Soon after the Polytechnique massacre, reporter Francine Pelletier, whose name appeared on Marc Lépine's hit list, called upon authorities to publish the complete letter the murderer carried with him when he committed suicide. This call went unanswered. However, a few weeks before the first anniversary of the massacre, Pelletier received a copy of the letter in the mail. With the consent of the editor, **La Presse** *published the letter in its entirety in its November 24, 1990 edition. Although its contents come as no surprise to us and do not really add to our knowledge of what happened, we nonetheless felt it would be useful to include the letter in the English edition, if only because it was censored for almost a year and caused such controversy when it was finally published.*

This letter is reprinted with the kind permission of The Canadian Press News Limited.

"Forgive the mistakes, I had 15 minutes to write this. See also Annex.

Would you note that if I commit suicide today 89-12-06 it is not for economic reasons (for I have waited until I exhausted all my financial means, even refusing jobs) but for political reasons. Because I have decided to send the feminists, who have always ruined my life, to their Maker. For seven years life has brought me no joy and being totally blasé, I have decided to put an end to those viragos.

I tried in my youth to enter the Forces as a student-officer, which would have allowed me possibly to get into the arsenal and precede Lortie in a raid. They refused me because antisocial (sic). I therefore had to wait until this day to execute my plans. In between, I continued my studies in a haphazard way for they never really interested me, knowing in advance my fate. Which did not prevent me from obtaining very good marks despite my theory of not handing in work and the lack of studying before exams.

Even if the Mad Killer epithet will be attributed to me by the media, I consider myself a rational erudite that only the arrival of the Grim Reaper has forced to take extreme acts. For why persevere to exist if it is only to please the government. Being rather backward-looking by nature (except for science), the feminists have always enraged me. They want to keep the advantages of women (e.g. cheaper insurance, extended maternity leave preceded by a preventive leave etc.) while seizing for themselves those of men.

Thus it is an obvious truth that if the Olympic Games removed the Men-Women distinction, there would be Women only in the graceful events. So the feminists are not fighting to remove that barrier. They are so opportunistic they neglect to profit from the knowledge accumulated by men through the ages. They always try to misrepresent them every time they can. Thus, the other day, I heard they were honoring the Canadian men and women who fought at the frontline during the world wars. How can you explain then that women were not authorized to go to the frontline??? Will we hear of Caesar's female legions and female galley slaves who of course took up 50 per cent of the ranks of history, though they never existed. A real Casus Belli.

Sorry for this too brief letter.

Marc Lépine"

The letter is followed by the 19-name list, with a note at the bottom:

"Nearly died today. The lack of time (because I started too late) has allowed these radical feminists to survive.

Alea Jacta Est"

NEW AND RECENT RELEASES FROM GYNERGY BOOKS

An independent publishing house owned and operated by women, gynergy books publishes feminist/lesbian books, specializing in writing that explores acts of resistance — personal and political, sensual and cerebral.

» **By Word of Mouth: Lesbians write the erotic,** *Lee Fleming* (ed). A bedside book of short fiction and poetry by 31 lesbian writers from Canada and the United States. $10.95

» **Don't: A Woman's Word,** *Elly Danica.* A courageous and exemplary account of incest and recovery, both horrifying and hauntingly beautiful in its eventual triumph over the past. First published in 1988, Don't has become an international bestseller. $8.95

» **Double Negative,** *Daphne Marlatt and Betsy Warland.* An innovative collaboration by two talented poets (begun on a train crossing Australia and completed on a Canadian island), a book that redefines boundaries and images of women from a lesbian feminist perspective. $8.95 / 7.95 U.S.

» **Somebody Should Kiss You,** *Brenda Brooks.* Intimate, humorous and bold as an unexpected kiss, a remarkable first collection of poems that celebrate the courage of lesbian lives and loves. $8.95 / 7.95 U.S.

» **getting wise,** *Marg Yeo.* Women-loving poems of resistance and triumph. In her sixth book, Marg Yeo shares hard-won truths and "the fine delight there will always be for me in poems and women." $8.95 / 7.95 U.S.

» **unnatural acts,** *Marg Yeo.* Poems that deal with ordinary reality with extraordinary honesty, depicting the physical and emotional bonds between women. $8.95 / 7.95 U.S.

Please add postage and handling ($1.50 for the first book and 75 cents for each additional book) to your order. Canadian residents add 7% GST to the total amount. GST registration no. R104383120. Individual orders must be prepaid: gynergy books, P.O. Box 2023, Charlottetown, Prince Edward Island, Canada C1A 7N7